MW01093334

THE MIDWIFE

THE MIDWIFE

A Biography of Laurine Ekstrom Kingston

BY VICTORIA D BURGESS

SIGNATURE BOOKS · SALT LAKE CITY · 2012

Photos courtesy of Laurine Kingston, with special thanks to
Marsha Mangum, Nancy Nielsen, and Nina Vought for use of
child-birth related photos taken by Laurine Kingston. The jacket
photo was taken by Richard Busath of Busath Photography. Jacket
design by Ron Stucki. Interior design and typesetting by Connie
Disney. Thanks to Jeffery O. Johnson and Anne Wilde for their
copy editing. In-house editing by Ron Priddis, with proofing by
Devery Anderson and Jani Fleet; index by Jani Fleet.

17   16   15   14   13   12   5   4   3   2   1

Library of Congress Cataloging-in-Publication Data
Burgess, Vicky D, 1945-, author.
   The midwife : a biography of Laurine Ekstrom Kingston /
by Victoria D Burgess.
         pages   cm.
   Summary: Biography of Laurine Ekstrom, a midwife and
activist among the fundamentalist Apostolic United Brethren
and Latter Day Church of Christ (Kingston).
   Includes bibliographical references and index.
   ISBN 978-1-56085-215-5 (alk. paper)
   1. Kingston, Laurine Ekstrom, 1931-   2. Midwives—
Biography.   3. Mormon fundamentalism.   I. Title.
   BX8680.M58K56 2012
   618.20092—dc23
   [B]
                         2012009726

Contents

Preface

When I met Laurine Kingston, I knew that she represented the type of woman I had studied in my graduate research at Northwestern University and that her profession answered a deep personal quest for an alternative to hospital birth. I could not easily overstate the intensity of dissatisfaction I had experienced with my first obstetrician. In fact, I can document my subsequent search for a better way through the arc of my experiences in giving birth to five babies. I can now see that in each case, I moved closer to finding what I assumed had disappeared with the railroad, which is to say midwives. I was in my mid-thirties and about to deliver my last child when I met Ronna Hand, an associate of Laurine's, and then Laurine herself.

I was so enthusiastic about my discovery and so pleased with how my last birth went, I applied to work for the Domiciliary Midwives of Utah and was hired to teach classes for them in the psychology of family relations and communications. My Ph.D. was in psychology, and a primary interest had been in the psychosomatic aspects of childbirth. When I met Laurine, she was already legendary as a driving force in the midwifery movement in Utah, and she was impressive. As I watched her teach and assist women in giving birth, I noticed how competent and cool she was under pressure—and I saw her as a role model for young women in a subculture that did not value them. I thought she was the quintessential Utah midwife, and she is! Whereas I had assumed my own life path had been unpredictable and colorful in its various twists and turns, her story outdid mine as a meaningful, adventure-filled odyssey.

Let me explain a little about myself and how I came to have this fascination with midwifery and with one of its key advocates. I was born in the 1940s in the little town of Salina, Utah. My parents, Fae Peterson and Stanley Burgess, were born at home. In their day, people did not know anything different. By the 1940s when I was born, things had changed and most everyone was born in a hospital, even in my case where it meant having to travel far from home. For those who are not from Utah, Salina was on U.S. Route 50, which was famously constructed through the middle of the state without touching any significant population areas. In 1990, Interstate 70 was built, which misses Salina by a few miles. Salina is about 150 miles southeast of Salt Lake City.

We were one of those sleepy outback communities the government disregarded in the 1950s and 1960s when it detonated atomic bombs in the West Desert, letting the fallout drift northeast and land in our gardens. Some of my neighbors contracted leukemia and breast cancer. I noticed recently that one-third of my high school graduating class had died—far too many people for my age group. The Atomic Energy Commission wrote a report that said they chose this area to test atomic bombs because people in the area were "low-functioning members of society." My father was a multi-millionaire cattle rancher with bachelor's degrees in animal husbandry and economics. All my aunts and uncles are college graduates. Governor Scott Matheson came from the county, as did the inventor of television, Philo T. Farnsworth. Utah writer Terry Tempest Williams has written about the experience of passing nearby when she was a child and observing one of the pyrotechnic displays in the desert, after which the fallout rained down on the family car. As a result, her family became what she called the clan of one-breasted women. We were all Downwinders.

Aside from radioactivity, Salina had benefits. I wore cowgirl boots until I was sixteen. By five, I was able to drive a tractor and could back up a wagon full of hay into the feed yard. That backing-up ability served me well in my later urban driving experiences. In fourth grade, my public education teacher sent me home and told my mother I was "mentally retarded" because I could not learn the times tables, which the class had supposedly spent all year learning. He said I had wiled away the time reading books instead of paying attention in class. When I arrived home, my mother took me down to the basement and told me to climb up on the wringer clothes washer. She told me I would not be allowed to get down until I learned the times tables. After two hours, we came upstairs. The next day, Mother took me back to school and re-enrolled me, showing the teacher that all I needed was a little motivation because I had learned the times tables in two hours.

I attended Utah State University and then Boston University, where I met and married Eric Olson, a Harvard student. After graduation, Eric was required to serve time in the military in Berlin, Germany, and I was soon commissioned as a first lieutenant in the U.S. Army Reserves. I worked at the military hospital. It turned out to be a famous facility where the Nazis had performed experiments on people. When I gave birth to my first child, Eden, I felt like another victim as the obstetrician gave me drugs, kept Eric outside the room, and took my baby away after it was born and quarantined it because it had a slightly yellow hue. My parents had traveled to Berlin to see the baby but were sent home disappointed, and even Eric and I were sent home to wait for the medical staff to cure our baby of what is, in fact, a normal phenomenon in newborns.

With our next baby, I made demands. There would be no drugs, I said. The nurses, who had never seen a natural birth before, winced during my labor. This was not very helpful. We insisted that Eric be allowed to participate and that the baby not be carried away after birth. They agreed, but put me in a vacant ward so other patients would not see what was happening. The staff thought we were crazy. Contrary to expectations, I delivered Erica without complications and then we happily returned home the next day. We were so happy and convinced we did not need the assistance of doctors, we decided to have our next three children at home.

In 1972, Eric and I were both accepted to graduate school, he at the University of Chicago to study Egyptology and I at Northwestern University to study psychology. My major professor, Niles Newton, had a research emphasis in the chemistry and psychology of breastfeeding. She was known to have almost singlehandedly brought breast feeding back to the United States in the 1960s when her research helped motivate the founders of the La Leche League. What she discovered was the role of oxytocin in human physiology. She called it the "hormone of love" because it contributed to sexual intercourse, as well as to birth and lactation. This had been exhaustively studied in animals because of their economic value but not yet in humans.

Dr. Newton was fascinated to learn that I had polygamous ancestors. She had also noticed that I brought my baby with me to class, breastfeeding her during the lectures, which may have been normal enough in Salina but not in Chicago. Dr. Newton encouraged me to study, as my dissertation was ultimately titled, "The Family Structure and Dynamics in Early Utah Mormon Families between 1847 and 1885." When I traveled to Salt Lake City to use the Mormon archives, I was told I could only use the resources if I promised not to use the word "polygamy" in my title. That was fine with me because a scholar would call it *polygyny* in any case, but such was the sensitivity at that time to a topic the Church of Jesus Christ of Latter-day Saints (LDS) was trying to put behind it. Things were more complicated than I can mention here because I received an LDS fellowship for my research, with help from Church Historian Leonard Arrington, who nevertheless would not let me consult the works of early Mormon leader Heber C. Kimball.

When the time came to give birth to number three, I made inquiries in our Hyde Park neighborhood about what my options were and was referred to a prominent physician, Mayer Eisenstein, who had become a home-birth advocate when his own baby was dropped on the floor in the hospital. Dr. Eisenstein said he would be pleased to be my birth attendant. Everything went well. Seth came into the world, I rested for two days, and the next day Seth and I participated in my graduation at Northwestern. Knowing I was recovering, the dean of the medical school escorted me across the stage. We all flew to Utah the next day so Eric could begin teaching at Brigham Young University in Provo, where my fourth child was born.

Trying to find someone to assist me in this birth, I

was told that Dr. Roger Lewis was unconventional enough that he might be persuaded to help with a home birth. My neighbor made an appointment and accompanied me, but was surprised by his attire when he entered the room without a smock. She asked if he was really a doctor, at which he hurried out of the room and returned a minute later wearing a white smock. I liked the idea of a physician wanting to meet the requirements of his patients in that way. He said he had never seen a home birth before but would be happy to assist. When the time came, he and my husband, along with our friend Jan Tyler (a godparent we called our goddess mother) and three children, all joined in helping me deliver little Abraham. Dr. Lewis was so satisfied with this, he advertised that he was available for other home births until he was opposed by Provo's obstetricians and had to retract this offer.

My husband and I returned to military service in Berlin, where we lived and worked for three years. When I decided to have my final child, Zachary, in Utah, it was then that I met Ronna, without whom I would not have been able to deliver a twelve-pound son at home, drug-free. Today Zachary is studying to be a nurse practitioner at the University of Illinois in Chicago. (As a proud mother, I cannot help but mention that Eden is a psychologist, Erica is head of a high school science department, Seth is a retired dancer of thirty-five years and now in nursing school, and Abraham is an attorney who spent many years in the army as a JAG officer.)

I have continued my association with Utah's midwives. My research prompted me to write *The History of Home-birth and Midwifery in Utah,* of which Laurine's career and activism constituted a major part. When I showed the manuscript to Signature Books, they expressed interest in having me expand on Laurine's life and write a biography of her. I enthusiastically agreed and spent about two hours at a time, twice a week, for a year interviewing Laurine, through her great patience and cooperation, and looking at the photographs and documents that verify her family history. We were thus able to piece together the facts and I was able to offer some interpretation to general themes that emerge as the major focus of her life's work. Aside from being an advocate for midwifery, I was devoid of any agenda in approaching this project. However, as we got to know each other—even better than we had previously known each other, that is—my admiration for her grew. She is not only a genius, but she is a model for many older women who aspire to age gracefully and remain self-actualized. I have tried to retain a degree of objectivity throughout the book, but attentive readers will notice my hero worship showing through at times.

1.

Beginnings

At age twenty-one, Laurine Ekstrom came home from work one day to find her cousin, Vesta Atwood, in labor and great pain. This was not entirely unexpected since Laurine's parents were fundamentalist Mormons and their home sometimes served as a refuge for pregnant women. Laurine herself was a Licensed Practical Nurse at LDS Hospital, although she had never helped deliver a baby. The naturopath, Dr. Rulon Allred, had been detained. He was not just a naturopath but also the leader of the Corporation of the Presiding Elder of the Apostolic United Brethren. Some twenty-five years later, he would be gunned down in his office in a Salt Lake City suburb by followers of a rival fundamentalist prophet, Ervil LeBaron.

On this day in 1952, everyone was worried, looking at their watches, but no one had any idea how to help.

So Laurine gathered herself and calmly walked over to the bed, put her hands on Vesta's shoulder, and quietly told her to relax. Almost immediately the baby appeared. Unfazed, Laurine did what was necessary and later said, "It felt like I had done it before. It was a calm peaceful feeling, like a hand fitting into a well-worn glove." She would later come to realize that she had the healing touch.

In the fundamentalist world in which she was raised, the healing touch was more than a metaphor. It was a spiritual gift granted to select women as a life calling involving the ability to transmit God's grace to a patient, although with the aid of technical skill. A midwife feels called in the same way that a man feels called to be a pastor or evangelist in the Protestant tradition. As a later assistant to Laurine, Kristi Ridd-Young, said of her teacher's ability with expectant mothers, "It is an unexplainable gift sense—a sixth sense." One can imagine a young Laurine discovering that she had this gift and could impart comfort and healing to expectant mothers. It was, for her, like being born again into a new life. At some point, there was no longer uncertainty about the path she would take. Her religious beliefs and single-mindedness contributed to her success and leadership in her field of midwifery in the modern era.

Despite the fact that the event in her parents' house that day constituted the first time Laurine had directly assisted a mother in giving birth, she had witnessed births at home, including the delivery of her sister Sheila when Laurine was sixteen years old. Sheila's delivery had been a breech birth. Watching Dr. Allred that day planted a seed in Laurine's mind for her career. She was in attendance at other times with mothers who were unrelated to the Ekstrom family. In her community, everyone knew that the Ekstrom door was always open to any woman needing assistance in birth, as well as to anyone needing hospice care at death. Fundamentalists were apprehensive about going to a hospital at birth where embarrassing questions were asked about the baby's paternity and regarding who exactly constituted a family member. The fact that Laurine's family cooperated with the Allreds and other fundamentalists who came from rival factions indicates the shortage of women at the time who could be turned to for help in childbirth.

Aside from being fundamentalist Mormons, what kind of family was it into which Laurine was born? Her family did not charge expectant mothers anything for the trouble of assisting their deliveries. Outsiders may have considered the family to be religious fanatics or eccentrics who had moved into the city from the backwoods. This was long before the return in popular culture to natural childbirth, organic foods, and the celebration of cultural diversity. But the Ekstroms felt like they were holding on to Old World traditions and returning to the purity, as they saw it, of a simpler time. Some background into the family's European and Mormon heritage will help explain the drive Laurine felt in living a double life, devoted to medicine and keeping secrets from her employer at the LDS Hospital and society generally. It would be a long, interesting personal struggle before society would come to sympathize with people like those in the Kingston group who wanted to take control of their personal lives and participate in their own medical decisions through a more humane, hands-on form of bringing life into the world.

Father

Laurine's father, Ernest Henry Ekstrom, was born April 19, 1903, to Swedish immigrants who spoke Swedish at home. They had a farm in Mayfield, Illinois, about fifty miles west of Chicago, and did their shopping in Sycamore, the DeKalb County seat, which was the nearest town of any size—not that it was all that much bigger than Mayfield. Sycamore itself had a population of under a thousand residents. While in the sixth grade, "Ernie" was forced to drop out of school to help in the fields. At fifteen he developed allergies, then asthma. Surprisingly, the doctor recommended that he pick up smoking to help him breathe better, which he did. Eventually he found that he needed to get away from the fields altogether for his health's sake, but at the time there were not many non-farm jobs to be found in his area, especially with the influx of immigrants. In fact, frustrated with this situation, Ernie joined the Ku Klux Klan for a while. He did not have any feelings against blacks or Jews, but he resented the sudden surplus of eastern and southern Europeans: the Italians and Czechs, as well as Poles, Serbs, and Baltic peoples.

At his birth, Ernie was christened into the Lutheran Church. As a young man, he was brought up to believe God was in the sky where he perceived everything a person did. In common with Midwestern Lutherans generally, he learned the importance of hard work, honesty, paying bills on time, and keeping his word. It was important to take good care of the few possessions one had and to appreciate them. People said daily prayers. As Ernie approached adulthood, this kind of training took hold of his inner mind to the extent that he found that, as a part of his general Christian commitment, he had an extraordinary empathy for people's suffering and loss. He became a Christian in deed as well as confession. In a way, this was part of his environment in that rural people in Illinois, who were of modest means, nevertheless shared what they had with each other. He found satisfaction in this, also in working with his hands and excelling at whatever he did. He maintained a realistic view of life and never romanticized poverty. He felt that too much attachment to material goods offended God, but so did self-imposed poverty. In any case, this was his general state of being when he received a letter one day from a friend who had left Mayfield for the west coast. In the letter, his friend told him that they were hiring at the

Ernest Henry Ekstrom in later life. In his youth
he was easy going and was able to balance spiritual tendencies with material pursuits, despite
his flirtation with the KKK. But when he met
Elden Kingston, it ignited a fire in him that
lasted to the end of Brother Elden's life. Ernie
was an accomplished carpenter, loyal member
of the Davis County Cooperative Society, and a
devoted husband to Blenda Frandsen.

Bluebird Furniture factory in Los Angeles. Like so many other people at the time, Ernie could not resist the lure of California.

Ernie was in his mid-twenties and not yet married, so he could not think of a good reason why he should not leave his home town. He said good-bye to his parents and hopped onto a freight train. He may have put some more thought into his plans because on that trip, even with clothes stuffed full of newspapers for insulation, he nearly froze to death. When the train arrived in Los Angeles, he sought out the friend who had preceded him there and recuperated from his hobo experience at his friend's apartment. Ernie must have been a sight at first with his hair matted and mustache tangled, and probably felt embarrassed because he was a short, proud man who was otherwise fastidious about his appearance. He was nevertheless easy going enough to let the hardship of his trip roll off his shoulders. He was outgoing and friendly and usually positive about life, which helped compensate, in making friends and getting along with other workers, for the fact that he was a short man at five feet, eight inches, and self-conscious about his looks. People liked him. He was immediately hired at the Bluebird factory, where the other workers soon came to respect his ability and dedication. Soon he was able to pay back his friend and buy his own food and supplies. Once those needs were met, he found another desire beginning to emerge—the wish to settle down and start a family.

Mother

Within walking distance of the Bluebird factory, at an industrial laundry Ernie found himself going out of his way to pass by from day to day, worked a young woman whose name was Blenda Roena Frandsen. She had a similar ancestry in Scandinavia and a similar rural upbringing, although in the West rather than in the Midwest. Her Danish grandparents had converted to Mormonism and immigrated to Utah, then to Idaho when Utah became too crowded for them. Blenda was just as adventurous as her parents, leaving home with their blessing to move to Los Angeles and live with her brother Allen ("Mack"). He had inherited a house from his brother Ralph, who had died from typhoid fever. Back home in Kimball, Idaho, Blenda's parents, Erastus and Annice Frandsen, were struggling to support thirteen children still at home out of eighteen total.

It may have been the circumstances of Blenda's upbringing and a feeling of being out of place in Los Angeles that made her the shyest person Ernie had ever met. In any case, he persevered in getting to know her and convincing her to go out with him. On one date, they went to a local fair. Even though Blenda didn't like heights, she was too shy to tell Ernie, who thought she was enjoying herself on the Ferris wheel and insisted that they ride on it twice. After the passage of a few months, they became engaged. They married each other in Los Angeles on September 9, 1928. It was a year before the stock market crash. At the time, everything looked rosy to them even though neither Ernie's nor Blenda's parents were affluent enough to be able to travel to California for the wedding. Blenda was twenty-two years old, having been born in Kimball on July 5, 1907. Her sweetheart was four years older than she was. She was the seventeenth child, while he was the fourth of six children. She had a strong-willed personality that might be called quiet strength. Reflecting his farming background, he was physically fit. With friends and associates, he was outgoing but would prove to be unassertive in family settings, less competitive in outdoor activities than Blenda's brothers, for instance.

The town Blenda came from in Idaho was little more than a wide spot in the road with a beet dump near the railroad. The reason the town had emerged was because the train passed by the farms in that area on its way from Idaho Falls to Blackfoot. There was a small church, a little grocery store, and a two-room school. One of the rooms in the school accommodated grades one through six and the other hosted grades seven through twelve. The teachers rented bedrooms from local people. Most of the residents were farmers, as in the neighboring towns of Firth and Shelley. Few of the young people finished high school because they had to work in order to survive. In this environment, all the farm labor and almost everything else was done on a family basis, with a high degree of cooperation among neighbors at harvest time, sometimes under the direction of the local Mormon bishop. In Kimball, about half of the residents were Latter-day Saints. In fact, the town was named after the president of the LDS Blackfoot Stake, Elias Kimball, who was the son of a prominent Mormon leader, Heber C. Kimball. Mormon or not, people in southeast Idaho were trusting and, in the absence of money, conducted much of their business on credit or by barter. The grocery store accepted eggs and other farm goods as pay for imported supplies and packaged food.

As she grew older, Blenda helped her brothers and sisters when they had babies to tend to or when anyone needed to be cared for during a sickness. She did the laundry by scrubbing it on a wash board and boiling it in a large pot on a stove fired by wood and coal. She was quiet and patient with this life and everything she found around her. In those days, work could be found by word of mouth, and she was satisfied cleaning houses, baby sitting, and cooking until eventually she was hired as a nanny in an upper-income home in Idaho Falls where she learned to fry chicken and bake fruit pies and keep the linen aired out. It was a simple and, in some ways, idyllic life for a farm girl.

This is not to say there was not a dark side to the town, where for instance a girl was raped in 1928 and the community's reaction was embarrassment for her rather than anger toward the perpetrator—much like what one sees today in other parts of the world when a victim is blamed for being attacked. The girl bore a baby and it lived only a year. People did not ask questions. They under-

Blenda Roenna Frandsen was an industrious girl who became a nanny in Idaho Falls. She was deprived of the educational opportunities her mother had enjoyed, but when she moved to Los Angeles she learned a lot about the outside world, preparing her to later live with Ernie in downtown Salt Lake City.

stood why the offspring of such an act might not survive. There were family secrets and unspoken arrangements in such a place, intended to protect outwardly good people. Even so, for the most part, it was a good place to grow up. Blenda hated to leave. On the other hand, opportunities, especially for a young woman, were limited there. When the chance opened up for her to join her brother in California, she jumped at it.

In Los Angeles, she was fascinated by the size of the bustling city and the trappings of modernity, like stepping out of a past era directly into the future. She enjoyed the novelty of it. Still, she always felt like a visitor and never really at home. When she became pregnant with Laurine in late 1930, she longed for the security of familiar surroundings in her parents' care. People in California were losing their jobs. No one knew when they would be the next to be let go. So, she and Ernie, who had saved enough that they were able to buy a Model T Ford, the iconic automobile of the day with a rumble seat and running boards, drove back to Kimball.

Idaho

For Ernie, Mormonism was a strange new religion. Not only that, but the State of Idaho required as much getting used to as Mormonism. The first permanent town in Idaho was settled in 1860, three years before the territory was created. It was about as far removed from civilization as possible at the time. Farming required irrigation, and rather than crops like wheat and barley, as Ernie was accustomed to in Illinois, farmers courted the lowly potato and sugar beet. Many of the immigrants were Chinese working the Snake River for a consistent, if small, yield of gold. In fact, a third of the state's population was Chinese through the 1880s. Added to that were Mormon polygamists who came from Utah to hide from federal marshals and a large number of blacks who started ranches in the West after the Civil War, living right next door to the Mormons, who thought Africans were an inferior race. There were also Shoshone Indians who as recently as the 1860s had fought white settlers in the Snake War and the 1870s in the Bannock War until disease and warfare reduced their numbers and they retreated to a peaceful coexistence.

This was the environment Ernie found himself in as he and Blenda came to live, temporarily at first, with his in-laws and then with Aunt Thera Nielsen, whose rock house was cooler than a wood-frame house and where there was extra room for the couple. Even at that, it was so hot the day the baby arrived, July 19, 1931, that Ernie spent all day hauling water from the irrigation canal to throw on the roof. The steam produced an eerie appearance like something from a fairy tale but cooled the house enough to be bearable for mother and child, as well as for Dr. Frank.

The timing was bad for finding work in Idaho. Ernie became employed with the Works Progress Administration (WPA), the federal agency that employed men during the Depression from 1935 to 1943. He worked, about ten miles from Kimball in Idaho Falls, with other WPA carpenters building an airplane hangar and airport administrator's cabin, both out of hand-hewn logs. Ernie did his own carpentry on the side when he could. All the while, he was trying to understand his wife's religious world view, which seemed strange to him. It was the first time he had heard of self-improvement issues like smoking being linked to theology. Nor had he heard of angels being resurrected humans or of God speaking to common people. Premonitions were talked about in Kimball—feelings that God was inspiring someone to act in a certain way or enabling someone to foretell the future— which was much different than simply taking guidance from the Bible, as Ernie had been taught. What he understood from the Bible was simply that he should be tolerant of other people's shortcomings and that he should be honest and fair with everyone.

For Blenda, it was hard to understand how someone could view marriage itself as a civic institution rather than a divine ordinance or to see polygamy as lustful rather than as God's plan for eternal families. So, the two held different religious views without letting these differences become a problem for them, at least for the time being. Meanwhile, Ernie found satisfaction in his work and learned to keep some of his religious thoughts to himself. He continued to act on Christian precepts in helping the less fortunate. It was a trait he shared with Blenda and passed on to Laurine.

Utah

As they eked out their living in southeastern Idaho, Ernie began learning more about his wife's family history. Her great-grandparents moved from New York to Illinois, where the Mormon headquarters were located, in the 1840s and then relocated to central Utah. Her great-grandfather, Duncan McArthur, had accepted polygamy and had three wives when he settled into Utah's Sanpete Valley among other Scandinavian immigrants. In Sanpete, they were so far removed from the urban centers of northern Utah that they often ran into difficulties with Indians. The seven-year Black Hawk War began and ended in the valley, the peace treaty being signed in 1872 in Mount Pleasant, which is the town where Blenda's ancestors had settled. Blenda's mother, Annice McArthur, was born there the first day of April 1863. When Annice's mother died four years later, her father, Washington McArthur, surprised everyone by marrying Eliza Rebecca Scovil, one of his father's widows. Such were the customs and society in nineteenth-century immigrant Mormonism.

In her personal history, Annice remembered Mount Pleasant as having been a bucolic paradise where her brothers would drive cows home at night and she would hold on to the tail of one of them, not wanting to get left behind. She said that whenever she saw an Indian, she ran home, leaping over tall sagebrush and never looking back. She remembered that whenever Brigham Young arrived in town, his entrance was the closest thing to a royal entourage, that one could find in America accompanied by town dignitaries and a brass band.

Annice's teacher at the district school was one of Mormon Apostle Orson Hyde's wives. Years later Annice could still imagine Charlotte Hyde calling the children indoors by shouting, "To Books! To Books!" When the Wasatch Presbyterian Academy opened in 1875, Annice was admitted to the private school. She enjoyed learning, excelling in algebra, history, and Latin through the eighth grade. For a while, she moved to the northeast part of town to be near the school; when her father became sick, she returned home. He died in 1879 at age eighty-four when she was sixteen.

The next year she moved to nearby Milburn to become its first teacher ever. She felt conspicuous because of her small stature, standing no taller than some of the students. This was not a drawback in the mind of Erastus Frandsen, a rough-hewn boy from Mount Pleasant who found her alluring even though he towered over her at six feet two inches. They met when he was nineteen (b. Apr. 13, 1861) and she was still seventeen; his parents had immigrated to Sanpete from Denmark. By the time his father, Rasmus Frandsen, and mother, Ane Margrethe Madsen, had reached the valley, his father—just like her grandfather

Duncan McArthur—already had three wives, including his first wife's sister Jacobina Madsen and a third Danish immigrant, Christina Larsen.

On October 28, 1880, Erastus and Annice took a wagon to Salt Lake City and were married in a temporary temple that was known as the Endowment House. Returning to Mount Pleasant, they lived with Erastus's parents for a while, but as soon as spring came they built a two-room log house three miles west of town. It was primitive there. They had to haul culinary water a mile from a meadow called Fiddlers Green or at times take their chances with irrigation water, but they were happy being on their own, raising cattle, sheep, and horses and feeding small flocks of ducks and chickens from which they procured feathers for quilts and pillows. Annice had thirteen children over a twenty-year period to 1900 when eleven children were included in the U.S. census. They attended public school in Mount Pleasant. Erastus insisted that the boys do well at what he had neglected for himself, sometimes beating them when they performed poorly at school. Annice, on the other hand, was a lover of books and read the scriptures and children's stories to her youngsters.

In 1899 Erastus pursued an investment opportunity in Canada and was impressed by the wide-open spaces. Even though the business deal failed to materialize, he began to think about moving to Canada or at least to somewhere north of Salt Lake City. They received a positive report from their oldest son, Victor, when he trav-

eled to the Snake River Basin. After more reconnais-
sance there, they decided to move to Idaho in April 1903,
meaning that the family of thirteen individuals had to put
their personal belongings, farm machinery, and animals
into box cars, accompanied by Erastus and six older sons,
while Annice and the younger children followed behind
the freight train in a passenger train. A month after the
Frandsens arrived in Kimball, their three-year-old twin,
Olea, became ill with diphtheria and died (her twin had
been stillborn), which surely made them wonder whether
the move had been such a good idea or not.

The Frandsens

According to the *Centennial History of Bingham County,
Idaho*, one of the first settlers in Kimball was a Mormon
rancher who ventured north in 1892. He had come from
the area near Bear Lake, an eighteen-mile-long water
source straddling the Utah-Idaho border. His name was
Jens Nielsen. Years later, after Erastus died and Annice
was still only fifty-five years old, she married the town's
founder. Jens was a ripe seventy-one years old on the day
of their nuptials. But when they arrived in Idaho in 1903,
she was a vibrant and happily married forty-year-old with
an equally vibrant forty-two-year-old husband.

The Frandsens stayed with neighbors while they
cleared enough land to pitch two tents and began erecting
a house out of adobe bricks. The father hired a mason to
teach his sons how to make adobe. Before long, the prop-

A family portrait with the founder of Kimball, Idaho, Jens Nielsen, in coveralls at the right of center (standing), and his wife, Annice Frandsen, to his right (also standing). To the extreme left (standing) is Perry, bookended at the extreme right by Burke (standing). Thera is at the far left (sitting), with Ammon to her right and Blenda in front of him (sitting).

erty looked like an ancient Egyptian construction site with clay-and-straw bricks drying in the sun, stacked into pyramid-shaped piles. Soon enough, the family was able to move into their new home. Before they had finished plastering it, a baby named Allen was born on February 5, 1904.

The family liked living closer to the town center than they had in Mount Pleasant, with the feeling of community spirit and cooperation they encountered. For one thing, despite being deeper in the outback, they came across fewer Indians. Occasionally, according to Annice, a Shoshone-Bannock "renegade" would stop by for food and she would accommodate the request. Sometimes the Indian would not leave and she would chase the visitor away, assisted by the family's German Shepherd and a poker from the fireplace. The threats to surviving in the American wilderness tended more toward accidents, disease, and natural causes than Indians. For instance, in 1909 their twenty-three-year-old son, Irvin, developed an infection and had his leg amputated on the kitchen table, then died shortly thereafter on October 26. Returning home from the funeral, Erastus and Annice received a telegram informing them that their son Ralph, who had been working in Los Angeles as a liveryman, had died of typhoid fever on October 29. There was heartache enough for the family, and one wonders how frontier people coped with the high child-mortality rate.

Isolated from the outside world, in times of tragedy

people in the Rocky Mountains often turned to popular antidotes for injuries and disease: home remedies whose reputations were based more on superstition than science. Annice developed a medicinal salve that became popular, made from rosin and beeswax, mixed in equal parts and melted together, then sweetened with carbolic acid and softened with mutton tallow and lard. Because of her invention, she was considered a healer and people would seek her out to buy her medicine. In fact, sometimes the poultice worked and sometimes not. It was at least a mild antiseptic and probably soothed the skin. She sincerely believed in her invention and often sat with someone who was sick, delivering a heavy dose of prayer and personal attention with her medicine.

Considering the pain of so many deaths, it must have been extremely comforting for Erastus and Annice to see their daughter Blenda arrive back in town and to meet their son-in-law. Probably, they would have been more pleased if Ernie had been a Latter-day Saint. Even so, they saw him as a potential convert. None of them yet imagined how dramatic a turn their religious lives would take. The Frandsens had heard rumors that a group in Bountiful, Utah, was starting a communal experiment like the United Order, something from early Mormon history whereby everyone shared their property with each other. At the height of the Great Depression, this came as welcome news, at least to Blenda's brothers and sisters. Ernie, on the other hand, remembered a Midwestern commune

A neighbor (left) stands next to Erastus and Annice Frandsen (right) at their home in Kimball, Idaho, with three of their children, Beulah, Blenda (black attire), and Lyle. The picture was taken ca. 1914.

that disintegrated when the group's leader, a Lutheran, disappeared with everyone's money. Ernie remained skeptical.

The Kingstons

When Laurine was about four years old, relief from the Great Depression arrived by way of three of the strangest-looking young men ever to have set foot in the town. Elden Kingston, Clyde Gustafson, and Marion Brown had long, braided hair and were dressed in a matching blue color. The reason they stopped was for gas *en route* to a farm Marion's family owned in the Teton Valley east of Rexburg. That area, bordering Wyoming and going back to the settlement of Star Valley, Wyoming, by Utah and Idaho polygamists, has always held an appeal for fundamentalists. While in Kimball, the young men met with Laurine's Uncle Burke Frandsen. They told him they were on a fast—not eating—to receive spiritual guidance. Ernie thought the young men were a sorry lot until he shook hands with Elden and felt something like an electrical pulse go through his arm. The more they talked, the more Ernie became convinced that Elden was someone in whom God's spirit resided.

Elden's full name was Charles Elden Kingston; since his father's name was Charles, the son went by Elden. When he was in his mid-twenties, he began to question mainstream Mormonism and, with the support of his father and mother, Charles and Vesta Kingston, founded the Davis County Cooperative Society in 1935 as a kind of United Order with fundamentalist leanings. Six years later he would formerly incorporate the society. In the meantime, his circle of acquaintances was living entirely in the shadows, avoiding any notoriety. Like other fundamentalists, Elden believed that God required him to live the principle of polygamy, which the mainstream Church had ostensibly ended in 1890 but privately continued for another two decades. The last polygamous marriage in the Salt Lake Temple was performed in 1914, for instance. The secrecy surrounding the continuation of polygamy made it look like the Church was not serious about abandoning it. It was said that some men had received a secret ordination to preserve the practice if the rest of the Church went into apostasy. The Co-op was not founded for polygamy, said Brother Elden, but for consecrating one's property to a common pool so that everyone would be equal. However, those who lived polygamy were considered superior, and those in leadership positions were expected to live the "principle" of plural marriage.

In any event, after the Co-op was incorporated in 1941 and Elden Kingston was subsequently excommunicated from the Mormon Church, he explained that he had sought guidance from God by going to a cave in northern Davis County, north of Salt Lake City and east of Bountiful, and that an angel appeared to him and told him to form a United Order regimen. The articles of incorporation stated the purpose of the society:

Charles Elden Kingston exchanged his farmer's
overalls for a businessman's suit and tie as he and
his successors built the Davis County Cooperative Society (DCCS) into an empire worth upwards
of $200 million and a membership of some 4,000.
This photograph was taken by Ernest Ekstrom at
Liberty Park in Salt Lake City about 1940.

To establish the long-looked-for ideal condition known as the Golden Rule: "Do unto others as you would have others do unto you." To abolish war and bloodshed of all kinds. ... To bring about the condition so that all incorporators are self-sustaining by means of their own labors, which labors are performed in perfect harmony with all other incorporators. To establish peace, good-will, and brotherly love between all men as well as all incorporators. To obtain, operate, and own lands, homes, factories, equipment, machinery of production, and raw material; all for the purpose of producing the every-day necessities and comforts of life for the incorporators. ... The corporation shall produce goods and services to be used by members, and to be exchanged with and sold to other cooperatives and the public for other goods, services, or cash.

When Blenda heard, through her brother Burke, of Elden's emergence as a religious leader, she had a feeling in her heart that he had been called of God, but she was less eager to jump into the unknown as her brothers Burke and Perry, who decided they would join the Bountiful Co-op immediately. Her brother-in-law and sister Ammon and Thera Nielsen and family were also soon on their way to Bountiful in the late 1930s. They turned over their homes and all they owned to the nascent Co-op. Before long, Blenda was feeling isolated in Idaho and missed her close relatives. She wanted to be a part of the United Order. Initially her mother, who had married Jens ("Jimmy") Nielsen, stayed in Idaho, then she too left for Utah, her late husband having died in January 1934. Jimmy's son, Ammon, had married Annice's daughter, Thera; over time, most of the families in Kimball came to be related to each other in some way. Now Annice wanted to live with her daughter and son-in-law, her late husband's son.

Ernie was not yet prepared to pull up stakes. Nevertheless, Blenda arranged for someone to come and pick up her and the two children, Laurine and Alton, and take them to the new utopia. They rode to Utah among sacks of wheat in the open bed of a ten-ton farm truck that could have carried a platoon of soldiers. The bed was surrounded by a wooden fence as if a corral were being transported, its human inhabitants substituting for animals. Alton had been born two years earlier in January 1936 and was five years younger than Laurine. She remembered that at his birth, her father had picked her up to let her peek through the kitchen window, where she saw Dr. Frank packing up his black bag, at which Ernie told her that her brother had come from the bag. Somehow, even then, Laurine knew the bag was too small to carry her baby brother.

Bountiful

The back of Marion Brown's truck was loaded with Blenda's belongings and sacks of grain when they arrived in South Bountiful and she and the children were dropped off with the Nielsens. Unable to stay away for very long, Ernie settled his accounts in Kimball and traveled south the next month. To pay their debts, he sold his wife's jewelry and other possessions, finding it hard to part with some of them. Even though he was traveling to Bountiful, he let "Brother Elden" know he would live the new economic order but would not take a second wife. Given the opportunity, he said, men were inclined to "plant their seed and take off." He would not do that. Blenda, for her part, was willing for her husband to practice polygamy and would thereafter occasionally encourage him, even suggesting a seventeen-year-old girl, Mary Stoddard, she thought would make a nice second wife for him, but he declined by saying he was not worthy of such a blessing.

The Co-op was not just what one might think of as, for instance, a grocery store owned by customers who receive dividends at the end of the year from the store's profits. In Bountiful, people were required to rid themselves of all worldly attachments, throw out all material possessions except for bare necessities, and even get rid of old photographs to sever emotional connections to the past. The intent was to create a new heaven and earth, beginning with the latter. Knowing this, Ernie sent some of the family's possessions to his brother Johnny in Illinois for safe keeping and for Johnny to enjoy.

Laurine's father worked on a sugar-beat-thinning crew that was jobbed out to non-Co-op farmers, accompanied by Co-op women who cooked for the men. Each crew had about ten men, of which Mack was in charge of one. Ernie was then sent to Elmo in central Utah where he spent the evenings sleeping on a board over a pig pen so that, as he said, he could protect the pigs and wake up early in the morning; in fact, it was the only place he could find to sleep. Nevertheless, the Co-op leader had other plans for the expert cabinetmaker and set him up in a home in Salt Lake City in the early 1940s where Ernie was able to attract some outside business. He asked if he could hold the title to the house the Co-op owned at 624 S. 900 East, and Brother Elden allowed it. It was an extraordinary concession, due to Ernie's status as someone who had come from beyond the Mormon culture the others shared. Ernie became Co-op member number twenty, which was a great honor. Every family head was assigned a number that indicated his position in the hierarchy, starting with Elden at number one. Ernie was so pleased to have such a low number, with its implication of a close connection to the leadership, that he had it engraved on his tools, much like a basketball player's attachment to his jersey number.

Ernie's reputation as a master wood finisher spread beyond Salt Lake City to Ogden, where he helped construct the Ben Lomond Hotel and First Security Bank lobbies. Members frowned on this outside work but were pleased that Ernie was bringing in outside money. In his spare time, Ernie enjoyed making toys for children for Christmas presents and making cradles and clothes hampers for their mothers. He served on the Co-op board of directors. In time, he became converted to the religious principles the Co-op espoused and received priesthood authority to pronounce blessings on his family members, as fathers in the Co-op did. These were ritual prayers recited with closed eyes and hands resting on a wife's or child's head, as well as at times healing blessings. Laurine remembers that she received such a blessing from her father when she was nineteen years old, indicating that he had been initiated into the priesthood. She was not otherwise told what the responsibilities of this honor involved. In any case, Elden liked to tell Ernie how much he valued his opinion. When Brother Elden died in 1948, it seemed like a piece of Laurine's father died as well, partly due to the shock of the sudden death. The charismatic leader was only thirty-nine years old when he succumbed to cancer of the penis after his followers tried to treat him with herbal remedies and to burn the cancer away with acid, ultimately taking him to the hospital but not soon enough to save him.

Ernie and Blenda had seven children, four of whom were born in Bountiful from 1938-1942; the last child was born in June 1948 in Salt Lake City, except for a still-born child in October 1951. Ernie was disappointed at first that the first child was a girl. However, in the end, he came to be extremely proud of his four boys and three girls. Laurine knew she held a special place in both her parents' hearts, but especially in her mother's because of her likeness to Grandma Annice, whose hair was red like Laurine's, a trait that was not present in the other grand-children. The red hair brought a frequent tease from Laurine's father: "Red-headed gingerbread, fire in the wood shed." As Kristi Ridd-Young said it, "When I met Laurine face to face for the first time, I thought to myself that dynamite really does come in small packages and red hair." Ridd-Young completed a midwife apprenticeship with Laurine.

At some point after Laurine's youngest sister was born, an event occurred in Grandma Annice's house in Idaho that left a lasting impression on Laurine. She sensed from the way the local women were talking in quiet voices and bringing food to the house that something was wrong. There was also an unpleasant odor in her parents' bed-room. A doctor appeared with one of those ominous black bags. In the kitchen with her grandmother, Laurine could hear her mother in the next room call out in pain. Every-one's voice was hushed. Her father was at work in his woodshop but came in to confer with Dr. Frank and then cried. The elders came and dabbed olive oil on Blenda's head to give her an Old-Testament-style blessing for recovery. To Laurine's delight, her mother did recover. As Laurine grew older and became more educated, she real-ized that her mother had experienced an incomplete mis-carriage that day.

It did not surprise Laurine that her mother would respond well to the healing blessing since her mother was devoutly religious. Ernie was equally deserving of God's notice, Laurine thought, because of his wisdom and dependability. In the coming years, when they opened their house to anyone in need of assistance for birth or death, their home became something like a hospital chapel. It could not have been better training for a life of service than if her parents had been Christian missionaries in Africa.

References

Bingham County History. Blackfoot, ID: Bingham County Historical Society, 1990.

Burgess-Olson, Vicky. "Family Structure and Dynamics in Early Utah Mormon Families, 1847-1885." PhD diss. Evanston, IL: Northwestern University, 1975.

Frandsen, Annice McArthur. "Life Story of Annice McArthur Frandsen, given in person on March 16, 1935, to Lloyd V. Frandsen, grandson." Typescript, 1962, Salt Lake City.

Kingston, Charles William, "Reminiscences of Brother Charles Kingston," quoted at length at "Charles Elden Kingston," *Mormon Fundamentalism,* www.mormonfundamentalism.com.

Kingston, Charles, W. "Autobiography of Charles W Kingston," quoted at length at ibid.

Kingston, Laurine E., "My Hair is Red," unpublished manuscript.

Kingston, Laurine E. "Ernest Henry Ekstrom, #20," unpublished manuscript.

Madsen, Neil, and Pearle M. Olsen, *The Madsens of Mt. Pleasant, Utah*. Provo, UT: Lars Madsen Family Organization, 1967.

Solomon, Dorothy Allred. *Predators, Prey, and Other Kinfolk: Growing Up in Polygamy*. New York: W. W. Norton, 2003.

2.

A Fundamentalist
Childhood

When the Ekstroms first arrived in Bountiful, the town did not yet have street addresses. Houses were identified by the name of the family occupying them or of an original owner, as the Briggs Place, Ellis House, Staley House, and so on. Streets were designated Orchard Road, Mill Street, Barlow's Hill (now Center Street), Moss's Hill (500 East), Tuttle's Hill (400 North), and Turkey Shoot Drive, as examples. These were descriptive, or reflected who lived there, and there were very few street signs. At first, the Ekstroms shared living quarters with Uncle Ammon and Aunt Thera Nielsen and then were assigned to live with another family in one of the Co-op's houses. Later on, they lived alone at the Ellis Place. This was followed by a period when they were again sharing with another family in what was known as the Home Place. It was where Elden Kingston had lived before he moved to Elmo, Utah, near Price. During much of Laurine's childhood, the Home Place had been the center of the group's activities, where, for instance, the Co-op board met.

After living at the Home Place, the Ekstroms would never again share a house with a second family. It was said that Brother Elden had a soft spot in his heart for the Midwesterner. For his part, Ernie was apprehensive about the Co-op at first. It should be kept in mind that Ernie had not yet converted to Mormonism and viewed the world differently than those who came from a Mormon background. Rather than fight this apparent willfulness, Brother Elden told Ernie how much he valued his outsider perspective. He must have sensed that this gentle touch was what Ernie needed. Other members were simply told to obey or leave. Considering the immaturity of the institution and the fact that Co-op members still had ties to the larger community, Brother Elden was performing a delicate balancing act in keeping the group from splitting apart.

The children were sent to public school and mingled with non-Co-op teachers and children. Laurine remembers enrolling in 1937 in Stocker Elementary, a three-story, brick building near the center of town. It was overseen by Principal David Tolman, whose severe manner struck fear in the children. For Laurine, school was an unhappy place. Class work was hard for her, although she earned passing grades. She was ostracized because of the ambiguity of her religious affiliation and because she also wore hand-me-downs that stood out despite the fact that her mother saw to it that her skirts and blouses were clean and neat. She protected her brother Alton from children who threw mud balls at him when he wore his red winter suit. She and her brother could not afford ten cents each week for the daily bowl of soup the school served in the lunchroom, so they were shunted into another room where all the students who brought food from home ate. Even then, the children in the special lunchroom made fun of her home-made, whole-wheat bread and jam.

At home, it did not do any good to complain about such things. Laurine's mother was a disciplinarian who assigned the children tasks and punishment. It was not an indulgent atmosphere. Laurine remembers her mother shouting a firm "damn it" if the children disobeyed her. Her father would chime in with a cautious, "Now Blenda," even calling his wife "Babe" to soothe her, an expression of endearment that was unusual for a Co-op couple. Blenda seemed to be the stronger of the two parents, but she usually strove to carry out his wishes, just that she tended to go overboard. For instance, after a monotonous streak of pork and beans with bread and milk every evening for dinner, Ernie would get up from the table, go to the grocery store, and come home with a roast. On the other hand, Ernie could be formal and distant with the children, suddenly slapping one of them and then apologizing. Laurine knew that her parents loved her despite the fact that they did not say so. They allowed her and the other children to engage in conversation with them on a range of topics and express opinions in contradiction to them. The home was busy and noisy and generally happy. The thing that worried Ernie the most was that, with the volume of discourse, passersby might deduct that they were religious heretics—something the children were taught to feel guarded about.

At age ten, Blenda started preparing Laurine for polygamy, asking her daughter how she would feel "if your husband was playing with his other wife in another room." Polygamy was a prerequisite for the highest degree of glory, Laurine was told, but it was something a woman should keep to herself. "Even if an angel appears and asks if you are a plural wife," she was told, "you are to deny it." Laurine had a sense of which women were connected to which husbands because when two families shared a house, often it was a sister-wife and her children in the other half. In such situations, each wife had her own bedroom. Plural families living in the same house often ate together. On the other hand, some wives had their own quarters, and it was not always evident who was connected to whom. A husband might have up to seven wives, while the leader had up to six times that many.

In remembering her upbringing, polygamy is not the first thing that comes to mind for Laurine. She and her siblings distinctly remember the smell of fresh linen and the taste of warm bread and bottled fruit. She remembers their clothing, which came from the Salvation Army. In Laurine's case, for a few years she had a winter coat that was so thin, she had to wear a heavy wool sweater underneath it. This made her arms itch, so each day she had to decide what was better, to itch or suffer the cold. Being young and self-conscious, she would usually dispense with the sweater and sometimes the coat. The oldest of the seven children in the family, Laurine took care of her siblings when her mother was away on errands.

The only material possession the family had of any quality was their furniture. Ernie had made two beautiful kitchen cabinets in Idaho, one painted a bright orange and the other green, and brought them to Utah. One day the cabinets disappeared and Laurine later saw them in another Co-op member's home. She understood that someone in the leadership must have told her father to give them to someone in greater need, and he did, probably without regret. Laurine's parents were happy when they were able to share with other people. So it went from day to day as Laurine learned to distinguish between utility and entitlement, beyond a child's innocence to an internalized philosophy that one should give away as much as possible.

Trips to Idaho

For several decades, Blenda participated in a seasonal Co-op trek back to Idaho to help with the harvest on the farm of her sister Beulah and brother-in-law Bill Whitmill. The farm was formerly the property of Grandma Annice; Beulah and Bill consecrated it to the Co-op. The workers would leave every August in Marion Brown's ton-and-a-half truck and return in September. Blenda's two oldest children, Laurine and Alton, rode with other children in the back of the truck. Laurine remembers the sun beating down on them and the truck's springs doing little to cushion the bumpiness of the roads. Her mother was usually pregnant or had a newborn with her, and if she was not, then Beulah was.

The gardener and horticulturist in Kimball was Uncle Bill, who raised corn, beets, string beans, and sweet peas, as well as fruit. The aroma in the fall was wonderful as the children helped husk the corn and cut kernels from the ears and harvest the other vegetables. It was not a vacation. They arose at 4:00 in the morning and dragged long burlap sacks tied around their waists as they walked up and down rows of corn and picked only the ripened ears. The beets were plowed up and the women bent down and put them into their burlap sacks for transport back to the house.

The younger children husked the corn while the "big kids" sat on stumps of wood in the driveway with large knives that they used to remove the kernels from the cob, a responsibility for which Laurine felt proud. The corn was first scalded with hot water, then cooled in cold water to make the removal of the kernels easier. Then the corn was packed in bottles for pressure cooking, sixteen quarts at a time, over a coal stove. The bottles were soaked in a soapy lye water to clean them, and they were thoroughly rinsed before the fresh vegetables and fruits were put in them. The bottles were irregular shapes and sizes because the women and children had gone to the dump to retrieve used bottles that had formerly held peanut butter, pickles, jam, or fruit juice. Once filled with corn, in this case, and the tops closed, the bottles were put into a pressure cooker heated on a wood-and-coal stove and everyone knew to keep an eye on the gauge so the cooker would not get too hot and blow off the lid. When the dial got to the danger area, a child would yell, "Red, Mama, red," as one of the first words in the children's vocabulary. Under normal circumstances, the steam stayed within the parameters for about twenty minutes, at which point the bottles were cooled and carefully packed to take to the Co-op members in Bountiful.

Sometimes when Aunt Beulah was cooking at the stove, Laurine noticed cats licking up puddles of milk around her feet, the milk having come from her aunt's lactating breasts. Beulah produced enough milk that she was able to sometimes act as a wet nurse for Blenda when she had not produced enough milk herself—and such was the desire of the sisters to help each other. In the 1930s nursing pads had not yet been developed. There were not yet brassieres either, but simply loose cotton or rayon bodices, sometimes with a string to tighten the area around the breast. It was not until the 1950s that underwear in general, at least as we would think of it today with form-fitting shapes, elastic waists, and a system for measuring breast sizes, would be developed.

After the work was done for a day, usually late in the afternoon, the children would go swimming in the canal. To this day, Laurine cannot swim, but she would sit on the bank and sometimes float on her back. She could hold her breath under water but not swim. Even so, it was enjoyable to splash in the water under the shade of the trees. Idaho was a happy place for her, especially in summer. She loved her cousins and was too young to be aware of the hardships. To her, a supper, as rural people called the evening meal, consisted of lettuce and tomatoes topped with cream and sugar, accompanied by homemade bread and a glass of milk. Occasionally, their meals were fortified by pork or chicken they raised themselves. The family seemed content with that.

Each morning, Blenda and Beulah got up early and breast-fed and cared for the babies, then made breakfast for the family and cleaned up the dishes afterward. They saw to it that the children were dressed and the cows milked. There were no refrigerators, so the milk had to be taken to the so-called milk house, a stone shed in a depression, under a tree, where the temperature was lower than otherwise and where they kept the windows open to allow for a breeze to pass through. Without screens in the windows, the flies, moths, and mosquitoes also breezed in and out of the little building. No one thought of this as being unsanitary, and since no one seemed to get sick, there must have been an adequate level of hygiene at the milk house.

In the evenings when it was hot, the children slept outside in order to take advantage of the cooler temperature. When they slept inside, it was just on a blanket spread out on the floor. There was a kind of hammock in the yard where Aunts Beulah and Beece (pronounced "B.C.") had tied up a box-spring between two trees and put a mattress on it. The mattress attracted bugs: caterpillars, spiders, and some mosquitoes. Laurine had to avoid the mosquitos because of her sensitive skin, which was sprinkled with freckles and often sunburned, a complement to her red hair and blue eyes. With the slightest irritation, she would break out in a rash. She and the older girls sometimes preferred to play indoors while the adults worked. The girls mimicked their parents' housekeeping and liked to help with the cooking and babysitting.

In 1940 there was a tragic accident. Three of the older boys needed to take some produce to Firth, east of Kimball, and two of the smaller boys went along, traveling in the wagon that had tire wheels and was pulled by two horses. Samuel, son of Beece and Burke Frandsen, was three years old and was lying on the wagon with his head out to watch the tires go around. When a car came from the opposite direction on the dirt highway, it came so close to the wagon that its door handle pierced Samuel's head. Laurine's brother was in the yard at Aunt Beulah's house when the horses galloped at full speed into the yard, the children screaming. Everyone was in shock. Aunt Beulah grabbed a diaper off of the clothesline to put on Samuel's head to try to stop the bleeding. One of the boys got on a horse to summon Samuel's mother, Beece, a half mile away. Uncle Bill's car had to be cranked and warmed up, so he started prepping it for the trip to the hospital.

As soon as Aunt Beece arrived, they rushed the boy to the Idaho Falls hospital, where he was pronounced dead on arrival. Everyone was nearly overcome by grief as the men began constructing a small casket and the women worked on lining it with satin and batting to create a soft bed for the little body, and the women embroidered roses for the inside lining of the lid. The body was displayed in the house on a table. The men brought in bottles of ice to keep the body cold. Samuel's sister bathed him every hour with saltpeter to keep him from turning black. Laurine was nine years old, her cousin Rachel twelve, so it was particularly traumatic to them. Laurine remembers the tears shed at the funeral, inside the house, for such an early death.

Aunt Beece, Rachel's mother, seemed to be frequently sick, but when Laurine grew older she came to realize that her aunt had been bedridden with twelve difficult pregnancies. In those days, no one ever said the word *pregnancy*. A woman was, euphemistically, said to be "in a family way" because it was considered to be too indelicate to say the actual word. In fact, Aunt Beece was a hardy woman who was fit enough when not expecting. She lived to be ninety-nine years old; at ninety she had a hip replacement. There were other things in those days that one knew not to say. Diarrhea was referred to indirectly as "the trots." A woman who was separated from her husband was said to be a "California widow." A stout woman was said to be "tallow." In the city, people preferred to say, for instance, that a woman had gotten her bustle turned around the wrong way. In fact, Laurine never heard anyone say the word *sex*. She also remembers practices that are now so archaic it is hard to believe that they were once normative. People thought it was wrong to wash babies with soap and water, thinking it would be too harsh for their skin, and were rubbed down with olive oil much like ancient Greek athletes except that the babies regularly got rashes from the oil—an irritation the mothers called "prickly heat."

The summer vacation in Idaho was never over until about a month into the school year, so Laurine would begin attending school in the fall in Idaho, and when the family arrived back in Utah she would enter Stocker late. Inevitably there would be weeks of adjusting to the curriculum and, looking back on it, there were hints for teachers to decipher about the educational conditions in Kimball—another reason for a cultural outsider to be pitied or ignored by teachers and other children. Laurine was always picked last for sports teams and could not easily find partners for spelling bees.

Life in the Co-op

Most of the Co-op houses in Bountiful had one bathroom for two families. Some of the houses were more primitive and still had an outhouse in the yard, without indoor facilities. Even though the Ekstroms shared a common kitchen with another family, they would eat separately due to the limited amount of space and to create the illusion of privacy. Yet everyone lined up to take a turn bathing in a round galvanized tub off the kitchen, filled with water they heated on top of the stove. Even in those crowded circumstances, the families managed to do everything with the utmost modesty, wrapping themselves in towels and ducking behind a partition formed by hanging up a blanket for a temporary wall.

From time to time, the Kingstons sponsored dances at the City Farm property it rented from the city, located near the Home Place on Turkey Shoot Drive. The City Farm was probably built by the Civilian Conservation Corps (CCC), which had a camp a few blocks away. The CCC was a Depression-era army of young men, in this case mostly from Utah and ages eighteen to twenty-five, who lived in barracks and worked on civic improvements: parks, roads, forest management, urban vegetable farms, and even zoos. The term "city farm" implied a garden or a place where city kids could come to see farm animals. Whatever the original intent, it was now a space for celebrating holidays with open-air band music and speeches, and the Co-op liked the property for celebrating the Twenty-fourth of July, the day the Mormon pioneers arrived in Utah in 1847, and in addition to dances, an annual Christmas party. For a summer dance one year, Laurine's father made lemonade, which everyone loved but thought was extravagant. Laurine remembers that at Thanksgiving every year, the Co-op pitched four large tents at Clyde Gustafson's property and sponsored a big pot luck dinner. One year, knowing how good Blenda's chocolate pies were, Sister Vesta (Elden's mother) secreted them away to her house, as Laurine discovered when she went there to play. To her credit, Sister Vesta made sure that all the children had a piece. Other women in the Co-op followed what they thought was the intent of instructions to save money by baking pies without any sweetening or thickening agents, to the surprise and dismay of everyone else. The rule was to eat and be thankful, no matter how it tasted.

In 1947, John Ortell Kingston became the second leader of the Co-op when his brother suddenly died. The members staged a three-day vigil around Elden's body, the room illuminated by candles, expecting him to resurrect. When this didn't happen, they took him to a mortuary and had him buried at the Bountiful City Cemetery. Ortell was in his early twenties, twelve years older than Laurine. Having known him since she was a child, she appreciated how sensitive and polite he was compared to the other boys. Now that he was a little older, he seemed to be a lonely young man. He would not marry his first wife until he was around thirty years old. When they were young, Ortell had taught Laurine how to play marbles. At some point in their development, she became aware that he had developed a romantic interest in her.

The young people in the Co-op were cautioned against kissing before their wedding day, which is something Laurine suspects was an easier injunction to follow in those days than it would be for young people today. Life was more family-oriented and centered on conversation and chores that were completed together around the kitchen table: sewing, baking, drying dishes, sharpening knives. There was no television and there were few movies. Young people were assigned a lot of housework. Rather than encouraging the youth to date each other, the leaders told them to seek a spiritual confirmation regarding who the right person to marry was. Getting to know the other person well was of secondary importance. Only men from the Co-op were considered appropriate for the young women in the Co-op. Curiously, women were expected to marry at a fairly young age, but no age was thought to be too old for a man. The men could find plural wives outside the Co-op, but if a girl married an outsider, she was excluded from the Co-op and shunned by her family. Marriages had to be approved in advance by the prophet, so if a young woman married an outsider, which the leader would never approve, it was considered to be the height of disobedience.

To avoid temptation, teenagers participated in group

activities. As Laurine remembers, it was a good way to maintain close friendships, something she remembers fondly. Her young group inevitably ended up at her family home to play parlor games. Looking back, she confesses that it did not seem like she was missing anything in life. She has pleasant recollections of her friends and the evenings they spent together talking and laughing. The others liked to come to her house since her mother fed them and was known as a good cook. Even if it was just homemade bread and jam, the young people appreciated it. She enjoyed the camaraderie, while keeping in mind that an important part of being a fundamentalist was self-denial and that her life was not expected to be all fun and games. She found life in the Co-op to be comforting and spiritually purifying, but she also enjoyed her friends.

The adult members often thought they were being tested by God to see if they would be fully obedient in "consecrating" (donating) everything they had as a prerequisite to gaining eternal life. Members were asked to commit to the following: "It is my firm resolve and fixed purpose to give my all to the Lord, my time, my talents, and all I am or expect to be, for the building up of the kingdom of God." This was taught to the children to recite in Sunday devotionals known as "memory gems," the equivalent of what was known in the Mormon Church as "sacrament gems." In this case, the sentiment was in line with what Latter-day Saints promise in the temple— a bit of early indoctrination into the philosophy of the

Co-op, taking its socialist orientation and making it into an article of faith. The co-op was understood to be all-encompassing, to apply to everything in life, even to giving one's body to one's spouse in marriage or sharing a husband with other wives. For the men, it meant confessing belief in the principle of plural marriage even if, like Ernie, one did not participate in it.

An irony about the Davis County Cooperative Society was that it was founded as the result of revelation but there was an initial reluctance to congregate for religious purposes. In fact, as Brother Elden said, "Anything that flies a religious flag will fail." Even though his father, Charles, associated with men like Joseph Musser who rejected the 1890 Church Manifesto against polygamy, unlike Musser, the Kingstons seemed to be content to watch for the Second Coming without trying to instigate it. Their only purpose, as they saw it, was to observe the admonition of Jesus to be one in every way. They met on Sundays in individual homes for devotional purposes without administering the Eucharist or ordaining officers. Elden and Ortell were considered prophets, and Charles gave Co-op members "patriarchal blessings," but that was the extent of the sacral overlay until the 1970s when Ortell realized the members wanted a Church and set up the Latter Day Church of Christ. What Laurine's family had signed up for was to be part of an economic utopia, in which they were pioneers, or even pilgrims, who were nevertheless unsure of where they were headed. All they knew was that they trusted the direction of their leader. For the moment, that was enough.

Meanwhile, soon after the Ekstroms moved to Salt Lake City, which was about six months after the birth of Laurine's brother Virgil in 1942, their house turned into a central gathering place for relatives and friends in the Salt Lake City area. Laurine liked being in a downtown urban neighborhood. It gave her a feeling of freedom that she had never experienced before, surrounded by people of diverse backgrounds. Their house fronted the busy Ninth East and had an alley on the south side that cushioned them from prying neighbors but gave them a front-row seat to watch the modern world go by. The sense of independence and the variety of people she observed made her life as interesting and educational as her mother's experiences had been years before when she lived in Los Angeles.

Laurine babysat to earn money and dutifully turned her income over to the Co-op, regularly paying a visit to the bookkeeper's office at 1700 South and 900 East where Ardous Kingston accepted and accounted for people's money. She was a sister of Elden and Ortell—in other words, a daughter of Charles and Vesta Kingston—and plural wife of Clyde Gustafson. She kept her maiden name to conceal her relationship to Clyde, as was a common practice among Co-op polygamists. When Laurine gave Ardous her earnings, she then let the older woman know how much money she needed for her expenses, and

In 1944, Laurine Betty Ekstrom (front row, third from right) was thirteen years old and attending Roosevelt Junior High School in Salt Lake City. Her teacher, Bertha Rappaport (front row, extreme right) is hard to see at first because she—like Laurine's grandmother, Annice McArthur, when she taught school in Sanpete Valley—was no taller than her students.

Ardous would give her that amount as long as Laurine's account showed that she had a positive balance, that she was contributing more than she was withdrawing. Like other Co-op members, Laurine was expected to meet with Ardous once a month to go over a statement of her account and defend how she had spent her money. It was something like the Latter-day Saint (LDS) concept of tithing reconciliation at the end of a year. Typically, adult members stopped by to see Ardous a few times a month with invoices, and Ardous usually wrote them a check on the Co-op account. Everyone had discretion over their use of funds as long as they could justify their expenses at the end of the month. If a member was maintaining a positive balance, few questions were asked. Members were not encouraged to think of Ardous as a loan officer at a bank, however. It was difficult to get permission for more than the usual amount. All Laurine thought about at the time was what an honor it was to be able to turn in money to the common fund and be considered an adult for doing so.

After she started working, Laurine was usually at school or work, rarely at home. She found she enjoyed the luxury of being able to buy her brothers and sisters Christmas presents. She came to realize that Christmas held a special meaning for her because for a brief moment each year, they did not feel poor. She and her mother made popcorn balls and candy and filled the Christmas stockings. Alton cut the toe out of his sock one year, hoping Santa would not notice and would continue fill-ing the sock with goodies. He put a bowl underneath the sock to catch the overflow. His mother teased him by putting a lump of coal in his sock along with candy. After the Ekstroms moved from Davis County, they went back each year to spend Christmas Day in Kaysville, next door to Bountiful, with Aunt Thera and Uncle Ammon in their newly assigned home.

One of the things Laurine remembers from the 1940s was that she bought a purse at the Salvation Army Store and found a dollar in it. She could not wait to turn the money in to the Co-op bookkeeper to add to her account, proud to have amassed a small fortune at a time when a dollar was worth ten times what it is today. In other words, over time she had managed to put the equivalent of a few hundred dollars into her account. She was so busy with work and school that she did not have a lot of time to think about anything else, but gradually she came to meet and become friends with some of the teenagers in the neighborhood and attend activities at the LDS church. She learned how friendly Mormons are, but that they can also be very nosy. They wanted to know why she didn't come to Church on Sundays. Did she belong to a different Church? they asked. No, she told them, her family visited her aunt most Sundays, she said. If asked to attend a particular Church service, she said she couldn't because she was expected to help her mother clean the house. Excuses aside, she had to admit that the youth activities were fun, especially when she tried out for dramatic presentations.

One year she landed a lead role and remembers a humorous scene in the play when she was supposed to be baking pies but was getting as much flour on her face as in the crust. The more that she brushed off the flour, so the gag went, the more flour she got on her face and hair. This elicited guffaws from the audience. For the duration of time she spent on stage, she felt like a star—someone who was accepted as a member of the community in a way she could not seem to blend in as when posing as a regular person. When her friends invited her to go to Church camp with them, she told the truth in saying she could not afford the ten dollars it cost to attend. There were a lot of poor people in the city back then, but she felt the sting of being on the wrong side of the divide between those who were getting along more or less alright and those who were not.

An open door

Already when Laurine was a teenager, her parents had opened their home to anyone who needed shelter or care. Her cousin Cecil Frandsen was honorably discharged during World War II with malaria and stayed with the Ekstroms through his convalescence. Aunt Beulah suffered from heart problems and eventually died from "dropsy" (edema) in their home. Laurine slept on the floor in the living room next to her and patted her aunt's back for comfort when her aunt groaned in pain. Beulah died in 1943. Her husband, Bill Whitmill, was left with young children. Laurine said that when Uncle Bill decided, soon thereafter, to take the children to Kimball, Idaho, "It was the first time I saw and heard my mother cry in front of her children. Emotions of any kind were not displayed openly," Laurine explained. Her parents never hugged her. A year later, Uncle Bill married a young widow, Lucy Snarr, who had four children of her own. One of them, Bonnie, moved in with the Ekstroms when she found work at the Sweet Candy Company in Salt Lake City. Bonnie had a hairlip, which was hard to overlook at first, Laurine remembered.

As an example of the cooperation within the Bountiful group, the mother of one family died, and when the father married a young wife who felt overwhelmed, the children were temporarily farmed out to other families and Blenda did the children's wash. Once a week the clothes would arrive in a car and Blenda would wash, dry, and iron them and send them back clean. This was done solely in the spirit of helping fellow brothers and sisters in the Co-op.

As carpentry jobs became more scarce, Laurine's father moved to Cedar City in central Utah, where he enjoyed the change of scenery and association with non-Bountiful Co-op workers. In such situations, he concealed his affiliation. Like a migrant farm worker, he spent his days at work and thought about home at night, sending checks back to his wife, who would turn them over to the Co-op and then send Ernie enough to live on. Ernie found there was a lot to miss about home: the aroma of Blenda's home-made bread and smell of the Postum the adults drank. Postum was a wheat-based coffee substitute that Latter-day Saints of all stripes liked because they could not drink what Postum imitated. Children were sometimes served hot chocolate. Occasionally the family obtained popcorn from the fields and popped it on top of the stove. In summer it was not unusual for the family to make ice cream with a hand-operated churn. Their neighborhood, southeast of downtown Salt Lake City, included the Dunford Bakery, which they liked, and the Tower Theater, where it cost fourteen cents to attend a movie. Occasionally the older children would indulge the escapism of a film at the Tower. One time they went to the movies with some Co-op boys in a farm truck that still had manure in the back: five young adults holding their noses in the front cab of the truck.

The young people otherwise had Liberty Park a few blocks away where they played softball and other games on its lawns and lounged under the sprawling cottonwood trees. In many ways, life was simple. They never worried about being abducted by strangers. The city was theirs to explore. All things considered, it was a happy childhood. As Ernie told his children, "Away is nice, but home is better." Laurine believed that. Sometimes she passed by a ramshackle house in need of a good cleaning, downcast people on the porch, and thought about how diametrically opposed her house was as a model of cleanliness and order and even of cheerfulness and a welcoming ambiance. Her mother frequently aired the bedding the way

Europeans do. The most uncultured aspect of their family was, according to Laurine's father, the volume with which they spoke. He still worried about what neighbors would think, although that did not stop him from sitting on the porch and enjoying a cigarette. He had not given up tobacco. To save money, he rolled his own cigarettes.

On the other hand, word was getting around that the people living in the house with the animated discussions inside were hiding some secret. In Bountiful it was an open secret, as people figured out that the Kingstons were political or religious separatists with more adult women than men in the group. In Salt Lake City, neighbors respected the Ekstroms but also assumed that they were poor and felt sorry for them. Laurine tried to pay attention to nuances in remarks her neighbors made and to decipher their meaning. As she did so, she became increasingly aware of the differences in her rural vocabulary and grammar compared to the sound of her urban neighbors' speech and made an effort to learn their pronunciation. She attended the public schools through graduation at East High. During her senior year, she found work in the kitchen at LDS Hospital and rode the city bus to work each day, along with a few other high school students who also served under Mrs. Springer, the hospital cashier. Laurine arrived home tired each evening between nine and ten p.m., finding it difficult to finish homework before falling asleep.

Later on in life, her grandchildren asked what she

did for fun as a teenager before there were cell phones and video games. She said they played Poor Pussy, which sounded scandalous to their ears. Nor were they impressed to learn it was a game that centered around a child behaving like a cat, whom the other children petted until someone laughed, thereby becoming the next cat. It did not sound like much fun at all to Laurine's grandchildren, with their endless sports and entertainment opportunities. Regarding the name of the parlor game, in Laurine's day no one would have said anything directly in reference to an intimate body part. When women were pregnant, they tried to conceal their pregnancy rather than let anyone know they were in that condition. In contrast to maternity clothes that accentuate the pregnant form, women in her day wore large dresses to conceal their distended bellies. Pregnancy was considered proof that, you know, blush, blush, a woman had had sex. Laurine remembers later attending to a birth on a farm and seeing a fourteen-year-old daughter gazing up into the sky for a stork. Laurine decided that when she returned, she would include the girl, with her parents' permission, in the checkup and try to teach her something about human anatomy and where babies come from.

Beyond high school

In 1948 when she graduated at sixteen years of age, a month away from turning seventeen, Laurine became the first in the Kingston group to graduate from high school.

She was sixteen because of a teacher shortage during the war, which the school district had made up for by cancelling the eighth grade—or rather by "combining" grades seven and eight. The war had brought other changes that directly impacted people's lives such as the rationing of fabrics, one of the results of which was that you could not yet find caps and gowns to rent for high school graduation. Instead, the students resorted to suits and long dresses. Laurine noticed how proud her father was of her, and he in fact told her so. Other members of the Kingston group withheld comment and let her know obliquely that they thought she should be working or getting married rather than going to school.

This, despite the fact that Laurine was giving all the money she earned to the Co-op. She splurged for a graduation dress, which was a beautiful light-blue color and had rose buds embroidered on it, and felt guilty about the fact that it cost fifteen dollars. Even though there was a dance afterward, Laurine celebrated with her parents over ice cream at the Garden Gate shop on 900 South and 900 East. Her graduation made her feel melancholy. There were parts of high school she liked, especially her class on nursing hygiene that was taught by a registered nurse. She was gradually discovering an interest in the topic, even before she allowed herself to think it possible that she herself might pursue a career in medicine. One day, from the school's second floor, she and other hygiene students saw a car accident occur outside. One of the students had a doll-like mannequin in her arms, and as she leaned out the window, the mannequin's head came off and fell to the ground, causing momentary panic in the crowd below. Laurine and the other students laughed. As they continued to watch the emergency medical personnel attend to the crash in the street, Laurine realized that she was not affected by the sight of blood. In previous crises at home and elsewhere, she had noticed that other people became hysterical in situations where she was able to keep her composure and think rationally.

When she was still in high school, she went on several dates with Ortell Kingston and found that she still liked something about the refined sense he had about him. She noticed that he was more comfortable around women than men, which may have been partly due to the way his mother, Vesta, had sheltered him. Laurine knew that Ortell's mother disapproved of her because of her ambition and, bizarrely, because of her red hair which Vesta considered a mark of the devil. For his part, Ortell was not interested in the usual dating activities such as going to a movie or socializing in a group and only wanted to go someplace in a car and park, at which time he would ask Laurine to sit on his lap and let him put his arms around her during their extended conversation. Once he kissed her, then quickly said, "Now, look what you made me do." Angry that he would be so disingenuous, Laurine told him she would not go out with him again. Whenever she thought about the incident, it made her furious.

When Ortell married LaDonna Peterson in 1949, Laurine thought it was the best thing that ever happened to him. LaDonna had been a good student in school and was smart and sensible, whereas Ortell was impulsive and idealistic. LaDonna would be the first of about twenty-five wives Ortell would accumulate, some of whom were from his own family. Like some of the preaching of early Utah pioneers, Ortell believed that intra-family marriages were authorized by the Bible. His brother Elden taught that the Kingstons were descended from one of the several wives of Jesus Christ, that anyone with a drop of their family's blood was special. It made sense to them to marry within the family. However, both Elden and Ortell told their wives and children that, in light of their divine heritage, they needed to emulate Jesus by serving other people, which tempered the arrogance that came with this belief. In Laurine's experience, the Kingstons were accessible and friendly with everyone else in the Co-op. The young women were dazzled by the trappings of royalty and considered it a great honor to marry into the Kingston clan.

It was interesting to watch Ortell mature in his position as head of the Co-op and acquire the designation of number one from his deceased brother. Gradually, the new leader came to see the board of directors of the Co-op as advisory rather than legislative and ruled autocratically as time went on. It happened naturally, not because he imposed his will on people but because they sought out his advice and considered it inspired. He, in turn, encouraged the idea that he was, in fact, infallible. Little by little, the board extended its discussions beyond financial affairs to family matters, civic issues, and religious questions. They would talk over an issue, Brother Ortell would make a decision, and the board would rubber-stamp his pronouncement. It was then viewed as the final world of both the president of the board and a prophet of God. His authority was plenary.

The Co-op had always given itself an overlay of theological justifications. Ernie was able to coexist with the fundamentalists as a Lutheran, but it was becoming increasingly difficult to do so. He heard late-night discussions at board meetings having to do with theological mysteries, alongside the mundane questions of investments and dividends. These deliberations were considered secret, but word often got out about what had been said. Blenda would ask Ernie when he returned home what had occurred, and he reminded her that he was sworn to confidentiality, to which she would reply, "Well, Lavona Rugg just called me and said her husband, Ren Stoddard, said ..." and would give a rundown on everything she had heard.

During this time, Laurine was working as a nurse's aide at St. Mark's Hospital, getting as close to the profession as possible. She consulted with Brother Ortell about pursuing a career as a Licensed Practical Nurse (LPN). He responded by warning her that education was damaging to faith and to good character but said he would not oppose it if she felt strong enough to withstand the secularizing influences of school. He said the Lord would guide her to know what the Co-op would expect from her in return. At the time, she was assisting a member who needed help cooking and doing dishes, and members liked her as a babysitter because she always cleaned the house after a baby fell asleep; but if she began school, she would no longer have time to work outside the hospital. Whatever Ortell expected Laurine to take away from their discussion, she allowed herself to understand that he had given her an unqualified positive affirmation of her direction in medicine.

For the moment, she was happy working in the hospital basement in what was called Medical Ward 101. It was where psychotic people were placed because they could not jump out a window. She was interested in what went on in the other areas of the hospital and was impressed by the competence of the nurses. She liked to hang out between shifts in the dormitories behind the hospital where the "cadet nursing students" lived. She thought their lives were stimulating if also physically exhausting. They taught her how to wash and boil syringes and dressings, which were re-used, and how to sharpen needles on whetstones. She was putting to use what she had been taught in her high school class, though realizing that nothing could prepare her, as an eighteen-year-old, for the trauma of bathing a 300-pound woman and discov-

Laurine Ekstrom at eighteen years of age. As part of an urban polygamist group, she was encouraged to blend in, as is evident by her stylish makeup and hairdo.

ering how many folds of skin someone that size has. She learned how to perform a bed bath for a male patient by strategically placing, then moving, a towel the way a masseuse does and handing the man a soapy washcloth to clean his genitals, followed by another washcloth for drying. When a male orderly was available, she was always happy to leave the bathing of men to him.

One day a nurse who lived in Kaysville was pulled over on the highway for speeding and, rather than accept the ticket, pretended to be in labor, putting a sweater under her blouse so she would appear pregnant. To her surprise, the officer suggested a police escort to the hospital. When she arrived, her colleagues obligingly wheeled her into the emergency room. So far, so good, except that the patrolman decided to wait for the outcome. After a while, a nurse emerged to tell him it was a false alarm. The pretend-pregnant nurse was warned not to waste the hospital's time in the future.

An issue that occupied Laurine's thoughts during her initiation into hospital work was the lack of dignity she observed during death. The person's family was usually encouraged to go home and await a call from the hospital. Feeling sorry for the individuals who inevitably died alone, Laurine sat with them on split shifts and held their hands, watching and learning. The dying, she found, lapsed into a halting, gurgling breathing pattern called Cheyne-Stokes, which is characterized by a period of apnea lasting up to a minute at a time. She felt like she could perceive a spiritual presence when someone was expiring. On occasion, people opened their eyes to focus on an invisible object in a ceiling corner or mid-air in the middle of the room. Once a Japanese man called out something an orderly who spoke the language said meant "Father, Father." One thing Laurine learned about assisting the dying and comforting the grieving was that the less she said, the better. Like a Quaker at a worship service, she waited for the intuition to know what to say or do.

Nursing school

Laurine chose to study at the Salt Lake Area Vocational School, later renamed the Salt Lake Trade Technical Institute and then Salt Lake Community College. The nursing program was four years old when Laurine entered it and was limited to LPN training only. The classes were held in an old laundry that was still being renovated. Twelve students enrolled for nursing training that year and two of them were older women in their forties. The purpose of the LPN program had been to solve a war-time nursing shortage, but it took some ten years to get the program off the ground nationally. There had been a similar attempt to increase the number of medical personnel in the country during World War I, with a program that had been limited to the east coast and Midwest. In any case, the nursing shortage continued in Utah, and realizing that there was a problem the LDS Relief

Society got involved promoting the curriculum through Church venues. Laurine and two other women were asked to accompany Church Relief Society President Belle S. Spafford to LDS chapels, where together they spoke about the nursing profession. The students enjoyed the company of Sister Spafford, especially riding in the back seat of her spacious car.

People have become familiar with the concept of practical nurses over time and know they work alongside registered nurses in the medical hierarchy; but as a quick overview, they are especially prevalent in hospitals, community health centers, assisted-living facilities, and home care. They can administer drugs, draw blood, insert IV tubes, and give patients oxygen, as well as checking vital signs, bandaging wounds, inserting catheters, and cleaning and moving patients. They cannot prescribe medicine, perform surgery, or diagnose diseases. The classes Laurine took in practical nursing were taught by two registered nurses and a hospital dietitian.

Laurine immediately took to one of the two teachers, Miss Mellor, who was young, tall, and fun-loving, while the other teacher, Mrs. Sandberg, was harder to get to know. More military in her demeanor, Mrs. Sandberg was imposing enough that Laurine felt intimidated by her—at least until Laurine noticed a pretty handkerchief in Mrs. Sandberg's pocket and realized that underneath her starched uniform and demanding style was a woman with a sense of fashion. All in all, Laurine enjoyed the instruction she received from these expert teachers. As part of her school experience, she was assigned an apprenticeship at LDS Hospital, north of downtown Salt Lake City, and at the county hospital twenty blocks south on State Street. In spite of the shortage of nurses, the LPN cadets weren't greeted with unqualified love and thank yous on the part of the RNs. Some of the RNs felt threatened by this army of young women in their blue-and-white-striped jumpers over white blouses, with white shoes and stockings, and went out of their way to remind the students that they were not real nurses and not even on their way to becoming real nurses but were probationary (called "probies" for short) and adjunct.

In reality, the probies were full-time staff members who were expected to work eight-and-a-half-hour shifts beginning at 7:00 a.m., 3:00 p.m., or 11:00 p.m., all without pay. They were given the most undesirable tasks. For all that, Laurine was happy to be able to observe the registered nurses up close to see how they handled emergencies. As part of the school curriculum, the students were moved from one hospital department to another, from surgery to pediatrics to obstetrics. In the Metabolic Unit, Laurine learned from the dietician how to make a pie crust and then how to measure the effect of diet on patients who had muscular dystrophy. Laurine liked the emergency room, where despite the fact that she was not allowed to do anything technical, she learned how to act under pressure.

One snowy night some gypsies brought a child to the hospital and explained that the boy had been sick for several days. They had given him gypsy remedies without success, and in fact, the boy died twenty minutes later. The head nurse tried to take the body to the morgue, at which the gypsies produced the biggest knives Laurine had ever seen and let the nurse know they would be taking the body. In those days, hospitals did not have security personnel of any kind. The nurse complied. Afterward, it was decided that she had done the right thing, that there was nothing else she could have done.

Laurine graduated in February 1951 and marched up an aisle with the other graduating LPNs as a young woman played *Pomp and Circumstance* on a marimba. The graduates wore their blue-striped white uniforms rather than black robes, but they were given a black cap and tassel and were pinned with a small gold caduceus, which along with their diplomas rewarded them for the most intensive year of study and training any of them had ever experienced. After witnessing the commencement exercises, Laurine's father suggested the family take a vacation and see their relatives in Illinois. He withdrew money from the Co-op to buy a new car, and then Laurine and her brothers, Alton and Evan, and sister Rowenna left with their father to visit the family's place of origin. Unfortunately, Blenda was pregnant and could not make the trip. Despite the extravagance of a vacation, the family bought groceries along the way and ate in the car to save money. The first time Laurine had ever stayed in a motel, she carefully made the beds and straightened the room before they left each morning.

After being greeted by Uncle Johnny, Aunt Hanna, and cousin Virginia in Rockford, the Utah visitors felt at home. The extended family lived near enough to be able to come and visit them before the week was out. Laurine felt like a country bumpkin compared to her older and more sophisticated cousins but agreed to go on a blind date with Virginia and her friends. It was a fun time and interesting for her to get a sense of the family's Midwestern roots. Laurine had never met anyone before named Ekstrom, and here now were three uncles, including Carl and Walter, and several cousins, as well as Aunt Lillie, with their distinctive name and facial features that resembled her father. It was a heady experience.

When they returned to Utah, some of the Co-op members complained that Ernie had bought a car and gone off on a vacation even though he had received permission to do so and had accumulated enough surplus in his account that the trip was insignificant by comparison. But people had also complained when Ernie bought Mentholatum for a sick child, saying he was spending "the last penny the Co-op had," so it was not the amount of a purchase but the fact of having or doing something the others did not have or do that caused dissatisfaction. Ernie had not previously considered that the leader of the Illinois Methodist group who absconded with funds might have been driven to commit this deed by the incessant jealousies and bickerings among the flock.

Working in the O.R.

With her degree in hand, Laurine found employment at LDS Hospital in the Women's Surgery Department, where she prepared people for surgery and took care of them as they recovered. For instance, she became an expert on catheterizing women. She liked the head nurse, Mrs. Potter, an older single woman who grew up in Tremonton on the Utah-Idaho border. Mrs. Potter seemed to understand Laurine and gave her a chance to learn new skills and even invited her to stand in on surgeries. Laurine enjoyed it and got so that she sensed the rhythm of the operating routine.

Some of the surgeons began requesting her assistance. There was a female surgeon, Dr. Lenore Richards, for whom Laurine had great admiration because of the doctor's precise suturing and other surgical expertise. Laurine enjoyed working with Dr. Alfred M. Okleberry, who assumed Laurine had come from an elite family with a heritage of medical practice. When she corrected him and said her father was a carpenter, he laughed and said that was no doubt why she was so good at assisting in reconstructive surgery. He was an unassuming man who arrived late one day after having done his son's paper route because the boy was sick. As Dr. Okleberry explained this, Laurine saw nurses' eyes rolling above their surgical masks.

In the area of men's surgery, Dr. Richard P. Middleton had Laurine help him with transurethral resections, or prostate removal by means of long instruments inserted through the urethra, through which the prostate tissue was burned away and then rinsed out. It was done under general anesthesia. The hospital had seven rooms for surgery, all grouped together, with patients' rooms on either end of the same hall. One day while she was working with Dr. Middleton and sitting on a stool in the corner next to a basin where irrigated tissue was collected, the doctor told Laurine she was in the right place because her name meant "corner stream" in Swedish, which she had not known.

Eventually she was advanced to the position of head nurse in orthopedic surgery, where her responsibilities included overseeing the harvesting of bones after amputations for a bone bank. She placed the bones in sterilized jars. Much like she had done each summer in Idaho, she made do with whatever bottles were available, often plain mason jars, and sterilized them in an autoclave. Stanford University, which had an exchange agreement with LDS Hospital, stored bones in the same assortment of odd sizes and shapes of bottles. The bone bank was no place for the faint of heart, any more than surgery was, but Laurine found it exciting to think of how much the preserved body parts would benefit the recipients.

She enjoyed her work so much, she began to think there was nothing she could not do and that perhaps she

By twenty-one, Laurine was head nurse in orthopedic surgery at LDS Hospital in Salt Lake City. As a Licensed Practical Nurse, she was interested in continuing her education and becoming a registered nurse, but her life took a different turn when she decided to get married the next year.

could become a registered nurse or even a doctor—or even learn how to fly an airplane. Years later, a helicopter landed in Laurine's back-yard pasture as the pilot brought his wife in for a check up. "How about a ride?" he said to Laurine. She told him she had always dreamed of flying. When they were airborne and she took over the controls, she thought to herself that indeed, anything was possible. For a moment she had really been flying!

Her success at the hospital was earned through long hours of work and little free time. Her mother helped by doing her wash and ironing her uniforms. As Laurine became established, she reciprocated by purchasing necessary items for the house she felt she could afford, while giving the rest of her income to the Co-op. There were more gifts at Christmastime. For herself, she bought a Lane-brand cedar chest to store linens and towels as she anticipated some day furnishing her own home. Every time she received a pay check, she bought a blanket or some other item for the hope chest.

A cousin of Laurine's, Ivan Nielsen, told her it was selfish to keep back part of her income, saying it should all be turned in to the Co-op. This was confusing to Laurine. She felt guilty even though she thought she was doing the right thing. Most young women in the Co-op were already married, and as she thought about it, the excitement of the hospital was not sufficient compensation for the loneliness she felt. There was no one she was really attached to, nor did she find any of the men in the Co-op particularly attractive. In a polygamous society, theoretically none of the men would have been off-limits to her if she had been interested in them, but she took her father's dim view of plural marriage. Her father had never really taken to the Co-op with the same single-mindedness that others had, especially due to the practice of polygamy. Two decades later, he was still his own man in many ways. Laurine admired that in him. Her father even expressed embarrassment over some of the Co-op members' attitudes. He found their approaches to architecture and carpentry to be primitive and short-sighted because, in his view, quality construction was always better in the end than something thrown together on a tight budget that did not last long.

All the while, Laurine had become convinced that there were good people outside of the Co-op. Within her subculture, this was a dangerous idea. But she was increasingly unconvinced by members saying they were "inspired" to do something. They could justify doing anything they wished by convincing themselves "the Lord" had approved it, as long as they had a warm, spiritual feeling about it. Instead of taking responsibility for the outcome of their choices, the members attributed everything to an unseen power over which they had no control. If someone expressed skepticism, that person was dismissed as an unbeliever and ostracized for "disobedience." With increasing frequency, the typical profile of a shunned member was a young girl who had not wanted to marry an

Laurine with her new husband, Leon, soon after their marriage in 1953. They spent their honeymoon at Yellowstone National Park.

older man. In such situations, the parents were told to treat their daughter as if she were dead.

Early on, some of the members had questioned Elden's authority in certain areas. During a time of uncertainty, Eskel Peterson, the father of LaDonna (Ortell's wife), dreamed his posterity had become greater in number than Elden's. Laurine was too young to understand this, but she noticed that Eskel stopped going to Sunday devotionals. She noticed, more generally, that the Co-op changed with each new leader and wondered how much it had to do with God's guidance and how much it had to do with individual style.

While she was pondering such things, the LDS Hospital offered her a scholarship to earn a registered nurse degree. She was tempted by this but decided that she was drifting too far off course and needed to realign her life with the objectives of the Co-op. She got married in 1953 to Leon Kingston, the oldest son of Elden Kingston. Her new husband had been the first member of the Co-op to graduate from college, and now he would be attending law school. The two of them together decided that, despite Laurine's scholarship offer, they could not afford to both be in school at once. Ortell foresaw the usefulness of a lawyer above that of a nurse, although he would soon regret feeling that way.

3.

MARRYING INTO
THE CO-OP

✵

Fundamentalist marriage is believed to last for eternity, more or less in accordance with the Latter-day Saint (LDS) teaching about the continuation of the family organization into the hereafter. And like the LDS, the Kingstons restrict access to the marriage ceremony to members of the faith. Because of this, Laurine was careful about her interactions with men at the hospital. When an unmarried doctor invited her to attend a hospital party, she declined. It was against Co-op rules for young women to date outsiders. She knew that if things progressed to the point that she wanted to marry an outsider, she would be shunned by the prophet and by the Co-op members. She also turned down invitations to marry fundamentalists from other groups, politely declining a proposal that came by way of one of Rulon Allred's wives, for instance. Within the Co-op, she received another gentle proposal, delivered by a wife of Brother Ortell, that she "might think about" marrying him.

Dr. Allred's Apostolic United Brethren (AUB) was one of the largest fundamentalist groups in Utah, based in Bluffdale at the south end of the Salt Lake Valley. Allred was someone Laurine genuinely admired, not just as a spiritual leader but also as someone whose medical philosophy was appealing to her. He called what he did "integrative medicine," or what is now considered to be a "holistic" approach, whereby he looked at a patient's overall psychological and bodily well-being and both counseled the patient and gave them chiropractic therapy. She understood the contradiction between what she was learning from medicine and what Dr. Allred believed about treating people with homeopathic liquids rather than real drugs, but his emphasis on nutrition and allowing the body's natural healing to proceed made a lot of sense. As she thought about it, she realized it would be impossible for her to switch allegiances and join the AUB, but she found that her views and Dr. Allred's to be compatible enough that she felt comfortable around him.

She actually preferred men who were older than her and more mature than contemporaries with whom she interacted in group settings. Sometimes her circle of friends would go out to a restaurant, although she was even more careful than the others to order inexpensive items in order to not be a burden on the Co-op. For a while she dated Wendell Owen without the security net of her group of friends. His father had remarried and moved in with a young woman, leaving the children in need of some help from other members for a time. Years later, as they dated, Laurine was appalled to discover how narrow his view of a woman's role was and realized she could not continue to see someone who was so controlling of women.

Young people were taught that marrying the right person would give them the best opportunity to go to heaven. They were promised that with "direction from a higher source," they would know who their perfect mate would be. In reality, the direction regarding whom to marry came from the prophet, who arranged many of the marriages, and from parents who encouraged daughters to take an interest in certain men. In situations where a girl was nudged into marrying someone she had not chosen, she was told that if they were not immediately attracted to each other they would learn to love each other over time. Girls often got married in their mid-teens and boys in their late teens. In a way, it was a kind of cure for the sexual tension that accompanies adolescence even if the marriages were often dynastic in character and depended more on who one's parents were than who one was attracted to. One day, as Laurine remembers, a girl was approached at work and told that she was to marry Brother Ortell that afternoon. "It was kind of a shock but something she had been prepared for" a few days earlier when someone told her the prophet had his eye on her.

She was taken to his house and married to him, wearing the same dress she had worn to work. He was thirty-five years old and she was seventeen. She could have refused the proposal, but in fact she considered it an honor to have attracted his attention.

During Laurine's stint in the surgery department, a young man from Egypt came to do his residency. He spoke English well. When they were in the scrub room together, preparing for an operation, he would ask the meaning of English words. One day he asked what "caress" meant. Laurine explained that it meant a gentle, loving touch. He told her it was useful because he was getting married soon; as he said this, she could detect a blush around the edges of his surgical mask. He explained that he was betrothed to a girl in Egypt and that his parents had arranged everything when the girl was nine years old. She was being educated to know how to talk to him and being coached on what his favorite foods, music, and clothing were so she would know how to please him. Now that she was a young woman, she was coming to the United States for the wedding, which made him excited but nervous. Laurine appreciated his confidence. She learned that Mormon fundamentalists were not the only ones in the world who were different from mainstream American society. Even so, she did not feel comfortable enough with her secret to reciprocate the young Egyptian doctor's confidence.

As she looks back on it, she realizes that she was naïve

in many ways about men. She was raised to think they were more competent than women, and she carried this idea with her to work, assuming that doctors always knew best and would not make mistakes. It was the same as her belief that Co-op leaders spoke for God and could not be wrong. Another misapprehension was that she was appreciated for her skills and for what she contributed to the Co-op and not just for her physical features. Dr. Allred treated her like a colleague, but there were other men in fundamentalism whose thinly veiled single-mindedness about marriage and sex was off-putting. She knows that she intimidated some men because of her education and career. She kept her house like a surgical room—clean and organized—and was always looking for better ways to do things. "Sometimes people in the Co-op irritated me because they were so darned stupid," she said. Some of them were uneducated and carried superstitious ideas, "which was hard for me," she admitted.

Leon

The day Elden Kingston died, Laurine was sixteen years old. It was a somber day, especially for the prophet's oldest son, Leon, who was fourteen. Laurine remembers how distraught he was. His father was diagnosed with cancer at St. Mark's Hospital, given electrolytes through an IV drip, and sent home to die. Members assumed he could not die or that he would resurrect, so they kept vigil over his body for three days. People in the Co-op were suspicious of doctors and preferred priesthood blessings and common-sense home remedies such as, in the case of Brother Elden, burning the cancer away with acid. Eventually the family called a mortuary and had Elden prepared for a funeral and then buried.

The leader left many wives and young children behind. Leon's mother, Ethel Matilda Gustafson, had a three-month-old baby. Laurine remembers that she was an "elegant woman" who had a remarkable ability to keep her dignity even with young children around. Elden had given his brother Ortell a verbal commission of the "keys of authority" so that Ortell could give blessings and run the Co-op, but at first Ortell felt inexperienced and lacking in the "spiritual strength" he would need to take on full responsibility for the group, so for a while Clyde Gustafson ran the affairs of the Co-op and conducted Sunday meetings. Clyde was close to Laurine's father, Ernest Ekstrom, perhaps due to their Swedish heritage and common language, so Ernie was pleased with the way the transition was being carried out. Over time, Ortell developed the self-assurance he needed as people placed their confidence and trust in his advice. He came to believe that he spoke for God, and the followers came to believe that he did.

Before dying, Brother Elden told his wife, Ethel, he thought his oldest son should go to school and become an attorney. The reason Leon was singled out was his bookishness. Where other children preferred to play sports or hang out with friends, Leon preferred to stay indoors and do crossword puzzles no one else was able to solve. There was controversy among the elders about sponsoring the boy's education, mainly because they felt that graduate school cost so much, it would deplete the Co-op's resources. The fourteen-year-old was eager to do what the group thought was best. What he did not yet know was that there are people who are impossible to please, who will give young people contradictory messages and little support and then wonder why they fail.

Time passed quickly. Before Laurine knew it, she was twenty-two years old. Leon was twenty and, in fulfillment of his father's prophecy, attending the University of Utah as an undergraduate. Ethel was doing her best to keep food on the table by working at the Co-op's shoe store in Bountiful and taking in Co-op teenagers as boarders. Her family was quartered at the Home Place, the center of the Co-op's activities and where Sunday meetings were held, for instance. It had a large barn, a cow that furnished the family with milk, and a small reservoir supplying water for cherry, pear, and peach trees.

As Leon was growing up, he tried to help the family financially by getting a paper route and working for local farmers. However, when he began attending college, he boarded at an old house at the Co-op coal yard in Salt Lake City on 3900 South 300 West where his stepmother Marion was the bookkeeper. The men brought coal in every day from the Co-op mine in Orangeville, southeast of Price, and other men collected the coal at the depot and delivered it to homes and businesses. Leon would help with deliveries after school. Even with so many distractions, he persisted at his studies and graduated in 1958 from law school. He had proven himself in an environment that was foreign to him by applying his keen sense of memory to the subject and disciplining his time. It was easier than it would be for most students, but clearly he had an aptitude for learning.

Laurine's brother Alton worked at the coal yard and became friends with Leon, sometimes bringing him home for dinner and to stay the night. "I have never seen anyone go to sleep as fast as Leon does," Alton would say. No doubt, it was the student's tight schedule that was partly responsible for his slight narcolepsy. Laurine had a similarly busy schedule and was not always home when Alton and Leon appeared, nor she did not think much about the visitor who would later capture her fancy because at the time, he was her younger brother's friend.

By the time their relationship came to a natural conclusion, their romance had already acquired a fairy-tale quality to it. The day fate was in their favor was when a big lump of coal fell on Leon's foot and his big toe swelled up to a size he would not have thought possible, accompanied by intense pain. Alton called to ask what they should do. Laurine answered that, "Oh, I know something about that," because she had seen Dr. Allred treat a toe that was in a similar shape. Alton picked her up and took her to the coal yard, where she heated a paperclip in a flame and used it to melt a hole through the toe nail, at which the pressure from the buildup of blood underneath the nail was immediately relieved. Leon was transferred to his mother's house in Bountiful to recuperate. Laurine followed him there a day later to change the dressing. While wrapping the toe, she chatted with Leon and was impressed by his intelligence and deep inner sense of compassion and honesty. It was unusual at the time for a woman to be attracted to a younger man. Laurine didn't know what to think at first, but Leon was the only man in the Co-op she had ever felt such a strong attraction to. Maybe the intimacy of dressing his foot helped break the ice. In some ways he resembled Laurine's father. Leon was a short man at five feet seven inches. At five feet two inches, Laurine felt at home under his protective wing.

First there was the matter of Leon's other girlfriend, Ruth Stoddard, that had to be addressed. Ruth came from a prominent Co-op family. The two had been dancing together a few times at the Rainbow Garden in Salt Lake City. Leon was considered one of the most eligible bachelors at the time, being the founder's oldest son, and could have continued to date Ruth as well as Laurine, but he was more like Laurine's father than his own in his approach to polygamy, which made him uncomfortable. So from the time he let Laurine fix his toe in March 1953, he began spending progressively less time with Ruth and more with Laurine. This was a development that Ernie and Blenda were pleased with because they liked Leon and his mother. Ethel, Clyde Gustafson's sister, was one of those rare individuals who accepted everyone without judgment and exuded warmth and enthusiasm to everyone. Ernie had helped Ethel with a few repairs at her home; he would later remodel her kitchen without charging her anything for his labor.

As a good Co-op member, Laurine went to see Brother Ortell for permission to marry, following on the heels of Leon's consultation with his uncle. The pronouncement from the oracle, as he sat uncomfortably behind his desk, was that she was going to break someone's heart no matter what was decided, clearly referring to himself. Leon's interview had not been any more satisfying because Ortell wanted him to divulge details about his supposed intimacy with Ruth. But Leon had not been intimate with Ruth. He later heard that this was an assumption the leader made about every couple that came for pre-nuptial council. There was a general preoccupation with sex, Laurine thought, as was evident in a revelation LaDonna, Ortell's first wife, received that she was to protect her sons' reproductive organs at all times, leading her to create loose-fitting, unrestrictive diapers and pants for them. Her sons would go on to sire over 106 children, so maybe there was something to the improbable revelation.

The happy couple tried to put the disorienting experience with Brother Ortell behind them as they planned for an August 15, 1953, wedding, which was scheduled to allow them some time together before school started in

September. Laurine sensed that her father felt an elevation in status through her marriage to someone so near the top of the leadership. For all of the usual reasons about protecting the Co-op from transparency, it was assumed that the wedding would be held in a member's home, but Laurine felt she needed to include her acquaintances from the medical world. After all, she and Leon were not getting married illegally. So she invited the surgery crew, who were ecstatic for her. No one was told about the Davis County Cooperative Society. All anyone knew was that she was the youngest person on the surgery crew and one of the few who were not yet married.

When Dr. Okleberry found out that Leon was studying to be an attorney, he said with a laugh that it was a good thing Laurine was getting married before her husband became corrupt. Mrs. Okleberry threw a bridal shower for Laurine, at which the bride-to-be tasted her first angel food cake. Laurine still remembers the scrumptious flavor of the strawberries, accented by whipped cream with small peanut-brittle pieces blended into it. She also remembers being at work that week and being asked by a doctor what she would do if her husband presented her with an orchid. She said she would thank him and maybe comment on how nice it smelled, not yet knowing that this was medical humor that drew on the words *orchidectomy* (surgical excision of a testicle), *orchiepididymitis* (inflammation of a testicle), and *cryptorchidism* (a missing testicle). They all laughed. In retrospect,

Laurine is surprised that with the inevitable jadedness that crept in after years of exposure to naked bodies and internal organs, there was not more salacious humor in the surgical room. This was as explicit as anyone ever got. If someone happened to slip up and use a mildly profane word, they would always pardon themselves.

Leon and Laurine asked LDS Bishop Amby Briggs to marry them at Brother Clyde's house in Bountiful. The bishop knew they were fundamentalists but was gracious in accepting the request, just as he would have been with an LDS couple. Leon, Laurine, and a few family members arrived at Clyde Gustafson's house a few hours early for the sacred fundamentalist wedding ceremony. Laurine's father read the liturgy off a piece of paper. Right before the wedding, as Laurine was getting into her dress, Marion stopped by to inform her that "the boss says it's not too late for you to change your mind," which bothered Laurine. She decided she would not let this inappropriateness spoil her wedding and put it out of her mind. After the secret ceremony was successfully carried out, Bishop Briggs arrived to perform the civil ceremony that would allow the Kingstons to receive a marriage certificate.

For the reception, Laurine's parents rented a hall at the Blind Center in Salt Lake City where Ralph Frandsen, the son of Aunt Lamonda and Uncle Mac, was enrolled for school and therapy. Setting another record for the Co-op, Leon and Laurine were the first couple to have a reception line at a wedding or to invite outsiders. The

The world looked bright in 1958 when Laurine's husband, Leon Kingston, graduated from law school at the University of Utah. The traditional black cap and gown had twice eluded Laurine, whose high school graduation involved a blue dress, her college graduation a white dress.

refreshments were limited to lemonade with ice cream, without cake, but Laurine was fine with that. Her dress was made by Leon's sister Eldean and the bridesmaids' dresses were sewn by Leon's mother.

After the reception, the newlyweds left for a one-week honeymoon to Yellowstone Park in Wyoming, driving her father's car to Kimball, Idaho, where their cousin Cecil Frandsen and wife, Bessy, insisted they take their Nash Rambler the rest of the way. The car was enormous and looked like a big blimp. It was manufactured by the Nash-Kelvinator Corporation, the same company that made refrigerators. Despite its looks, it came in handy because the front and back seats folded down into a bed, meaning that the couple did not need to rent motel rooms. So, off they went to the park, much like Laurine's parents did when they traveled to Idaho in their new Model T after their marriage. The weather was perfect and the scenery was beautiful. They ate simply and bathed in streams, proving the message the Co-op promoted, that a rich man has all he needs, but he needs very little.

When they returned home, they stayed with Laurine's parents for a month, then rented a small basement apartment near LDS Hospital at 422 Eighth Avenue. Rent was $35.00 a month including utilities. There was a garage for the car Leon inherited from his father, a boxy 1940 Plymouth that they said, laughingly, was held together with bailing wire. It was Leon's means of getting to and from law school during the week and to the coal yard on weekends.

Everyone in surgery was glad to see Laurine back, safe and sound. When they asked her what she had done all week in Yellowstone, she said she had "played with the bears, … among other things," which elicited some giggles. The unexpected news was that Leon was teaching Laurine how to drive. This news was received well by the people in the surgical unit, but in the Co-op it represented a huge step forward for a woman. Neither Leon's nor Laurine's mothers had ever driven a car. The thinking was that if Laurine obtained a drivers license, she would be able to do the shopping on her own. In addition, their apartment did not have a washing machine, so Laurine had to take the laundry to her parents' house by putting it in a stroller and taking a steep, two-mile hike down the hill, out of the avenues, to the 900 East neighborhood and then get a ride back with Leon in the evening. The sooner she could learn how to drive, the better.

Their little apartment on Eighth Avenue was connected to an even smaller studio apartment by a locked door, where another couple lived. When their first baby arrived in about two years, their landlord expanded the apartment by opening up the door into the studio and combining the two. They were surprised that a child had not come sooner because they had not used birth control. In fact, before the baby arrived, they were hyper-conscious of how quiet and lonely their apartment seemed. It was the first time in Laurine's life that she had lived in a house without children underfoot. The couple decided to buy two parakeets to fill the silent void, and when the birds had babies almost immediately, it seemed like they were being mocked. But eventually Laurine conceived and their first child, a boy, was born in June 1955. Laurine took three weeks off to recover and then went back to work. Her mother tended the baby during work hours, so Laurine embarked on a very modern way of juggling work and children.

They had not planned on it, but a girl baby was born the very next year in October 1956. Laurine kept working, spending her evenings hand-washing cloth diapers in the sink so she could give her mother a fresh stack of clean nappies every morning. She didn't seem to notice at the time how demanding it was having two children under the age of two. "The great thing about youth is that few things seem as important as the happiness you're experiencing," she reminisced.

The coal yard

Their happiness would be interrupted to a degree when the Co-op told them they had two days to move from their apartment in the avenues to a house at the coal yard at 197 West 3900 South. The family living there was told to move elsewhere. Leon and Laurine found the house to be a disaster, but Laurine's father came to the rescue to help repair walls and update old and inadequate fixtures. He found an unplumbed kitchen sink that emptied straight into the dirt under the house, which explained the bad odor that had permeated the residence. Ernie spread lime under the house to help absorb the smell. He replaced the old electrical wiring. All the while, the Co-op let the family know they were spending more on updating the house than contributing to the common fund.

Laurine knew that she could not commute to LDS Hospital because it was too far to walk and the bus connections were not good; she had not yet become competent enough behind a wheel to trust herself driving. She gave the excuse at work that she had a sickness in the family and quit her job, then applied for work at County Hospital on 2100 South, where her application was accepted the next day. As she and Leon settled into their new surroundings, they came to appreciate the fact that this was not an apartment but a real house with potential for children: two bedrooms, living room, kitchen, and bathroom. The coal stove was a step backward and sometimes added a dose of soot to the air, which collected on the walls, but Laurine had grown up with a stove like that in Idaho. It was 1958 and the world was new, Leon having just graduated from law school. It was exciting to imagine Leon working in a law office even though for the moment he was keeping an eye on the coal yard and working day-to-day at the Ensign Shoe Business, a Co-op enterprise. Another reality of their new home was that its location made it a central gathering place for Co-op members in Salt Lake City. It was like living in a fish bowl with people coming and going for Sunday devotionals and weekday shopping. The property included a grocery store, Co-op gas pump, a scale for coal trucks, and a garage for repairing the trucks, all under the umbrella of a sign that read Valley Feed and Coal. The grocery store was closed to the public, but the feed store offered grains and hay for any farmer. Laurine and Leon tended a First Aid station, harvested eggs from the flock of chickens, and helped distribute money to Co-op members as needed. They were trusted, but they were also overworked. Even so, they knew they were not the only Co-op members struggling to keep their heads above water.

Laurine and her family were visited at their 3900 South home by Ervil LeBaron, second-in-command of the polygamist Church of the Firstborn of the Fullness of Times, headquartered in Galeana, thirty miles south of the Mormon colonies in Chihuahua, Mexico. Laurine remembers that he was a large man dressed in a wool suit in the middle of summer, who stayed for hours trying to persuade Leon and Laurine to leave the Co-op for his group. He said he would be able to put a midwife and attorney to good use in the Church of the Firstborn, but mostly he just frightened them. Saying she needed to put her children to bed, Laurine turned up the furnace; he began to perspire and soon left rather than take off his suit coat. The LeBarons tried to convince other people to join them and were able to establish a foothold in the Salt Lake Valley, leading to the subsequent tension between competing polygamists.

Aside from that, the year 1958 came and went without too much excitement. In December 1959 Laurine and Leon were blessed with another baby girl. By now, they had fallen into a regular routine of Laurine leaving early for work and Leon taking the children to Blenda for tending. Physically demanding for grandma, Blenda nevertheless enjoyed having her grandchildren near her. Laurine had begun to help deliver babies for the plural wives who could not easily go to the hospital, in tandem with a new trend in the country that saw doctors, even from LDS Hospital, begin assisting with home deliveries and a more natural way of giving birth. Perhaps that was why Laurine felt the timing was right to speak to John Brockert, state registrar and director of the Utah Office of Vital Records and Statistics, located in the Department of Health building near Redwood Road. She found a sympathetic ear, the director not having known that there were women who were not reporting births because when they came to register a baby, they were grilled about who the father was and the circumstances surrounding the delivery. He assured Laurine that this would stop—also that translation services would be provided for women who needed help with English. He subsequently invited Laurine to sit in on department meetings as a community representative. He knew she was a midwife but did not acknowledge this to her or anyone else because, as an LPN, it was illegal for her to practice medicine on her own.

The curiosity on the part of the government to know

a child's paternity had to do with a concern for thorough-ness and suspicion of fraud. The Co-op had encouraged its women to give government officials the impression that they were prostitutes in order to collect public assistance as single mothers. As a result of changes begun in the 1960s by both the government and the fundamentalists, a program allowed Utah's midwives to record births as doc-umentation for granting birth certificates. Today, accord-ing to Marie Aschliman, an information analyst with Vital Records, some forty midwives cooperate with the state in this way even though most of them remain aloof from the state's midwife licensing program.

Laurine bore three more children in the 1960s, begin-ning with a daughter in July 1961 and a son in January 1964. Her boy's birth was difficult. Laurine was in labor when she realized that things were not going well. She told her husband to put his finger in and see what he could feel, and she can still remember the ashen look on his face. "There's something there," he said tentatively, "but I don't know what it is." "Well, find out!" she snapped. "Oh, it's a foot," he said. "Okay," she said, "that means it's a breech. Take hold of the legs and guide him and I'll push when I feel like it," she said, and did. The baby was born healthy, to her great relief. Under normal circumstances, she explains, the prophet would have been in attendance at the birth, along with a midwife. Brother Ortell felt it was his responsibility, following the example of his pre-decessor, to attend to births. But Laurine would not let her husband contact him, so things proceeded as they did without his supervision. She knew that Brother Ortell became faint at the sight of blood anyway. Now his son, Paul Kingston, continues the tradition of attending to difficult births as a principle part of his responsibilities as leader of the flock.

When Laurine's last child was born in September 1966, she was feeling her age and bowing under the weight of the child. As her sister said, she was waddling like a duck. Laurine was sensitive about this observation but knew it was true. Her son was born on a hot day in a home that had no air conditioning. There happened to be a window near the bed at her mother's home, and she was grateful for the fact that a slight breeze came through the window. Leon was in New York buying shoes for the store. The birth was left to Laurine, with help from her mother and mother-in-law. They were nervous because all of them were used to having a man nearby, someone with priesthood authority to administer a healing blessing if he needed to. Laurine felt too modest to want to have Brother Ortell around her at such a time. She now believes women have their own priesthood authority, along with their husbands, to assist in births and give healing blessings. There are strong women in the Co-op who know how to take charge in such situations, but at the time she thought they were at the mercy of mother nature without a man present to intervene if something went wrong.

When the baby was born, he was, well, large—the

Two years after their marriage in 1953, six children came quickly to the Kingstons through 1966, this portrait having been taken in 1965.

largest she had ever delivered. There were complications when the placenta did not come out and she started bleeding, then passed out. Her mother and mother-in-law took the baby into the other room. By doing so, they left her alone. Things were foggy, but she felt panicked and lost. She could feel that the placenta was still in place, but she lacked the strength to call for help. As she looked back on this later, she realized that it was a wonderful education for her about how women needed the security of someone standing by, devoting undivided attention to the mother. She had felt like death was not far away. Eventually the mothers came in and got the placenta out. She remembers she did not feel better until she had nursed her new baby, that it was an important bonding moment for her and her baby. She wondered what people were thinking who took a newborn into another room, especially in the hospital where the mother might not see the baby for hours at a time, keeping the child separated so the mother could sleep.

They reached Leon in New York so he could hear the baby cry over the telephone. He said he felt like he had let down his wife even though he had not been given an option in the matter. The "Kingdom of God," as members of the Co-op called it, took priority over everything else. They thought that whatever they were asked to do, no matter how hard it was, they were to do their best without question. As Brother Elden once explained it, the "law of satisfaction" demanded that those in authority, who were making investments in their followers, be rewarded with undivided loyalty. Their original family patriarch, Charles Kingston, had received priesthood authority from the Mormon Church and shared it with other men. His son Elden received authority both from his father and directly from heaven when an angel appeared to him. He passed it on to his sons and to other men in the group. This view of priesthood envisions authority like a commodity that one can bequeath to others. The Mormon Church similarly sees priesthood as something one person can give to another, while the Protestant view is that an individual apprehends his or her calling and the Church confirms but does not transmit the authority or power. In the LDS conception, Charles's 1929 excommunication was like a merchant reclaiming something a customer had taken on credit and defaulted on. The Church was just repossessing what it owned.

Public attention

The Mormon Church was serious about corralling its heritage and collaborating with law enforcement in searching out polygamists. The LDS Church saw fundamentalists as heretics and ingrates who had once enjoyed the Church's fellowship—counterfeits whose existence devalued the larger Church. LDS leaders provided behind-the-scenes assistance in 1953 when federal officials raided the polygamist town of Short Creek, Arizona. Similarly, the Latter-day Saint hierarchy encouraged an

April 1959 investigation into the Davis County Cooperative Society (DCCS) and other organizations suspected of harboring polygamists. A request was made by
state Attorney General Walter L. Budge to Utah District
Attorney L. Roland Anderson in Ogden to look into the
DCCS. An investigation was launched, some of the Co-
op's leading men summoned to a hearing before a grand
jury, and the attorney general bragged that "his office had
been investigating polygamy for many years and will continue to investigate and prosecute."

Leon was asked to help represent the Co-op members
with assistance from Galen J. Ross, a law school friend.
When the district attorney tried to bring the cases to trial,
Kingston and Ross argued in the judge's chambers that
there was insufficient evidence to proceed. Since the state
had been unable to corroborate charges of bigamy and
had reduced the charges to perjury but lacked the wit-
nesses to establish that the suspects had in fact lied, the
judge dismissed the cases against ten men and women. In
the end, three individuals were convicted. None of them
were DCCS members. Two others left the state without
the court's permission and became fugitives.

After providing expert council in representing the
Co-op's interests, Leon might have been expected to
become the in-house counsel for the Co-op but was not
offered the position. He took on a few other legal cases
involving adoption and divorce, though without the support of Uncle Ortell, who seemed committed to keeping

Leon away from the law. As Ortell's opposition became apparent, Leon became frustrated and depressed. Brother Ortell's lack of confidence may have stemmed from the fact that Leon was young and inexperienced and shy by nature. Leon's strength was probably more that of a researcher than a litigator. But Laurine also wondered if Ortell's decisions were in part designed to keep Leon at arm's length from the center of the Church bureaucracy. It was common to put a ceiling on someone's influence who was thought to be a potential threat to the leadership. Leon's involvement with the shoe business was important, but even there he was mostly expected to perform menial tasks at never more than eight dollars per hour. Ortell's opinion may have been influenced by the fact that a week after the legal issues were settled, Leon developed bleeding ulcers and black stools. When Laurine noticed the aroma of blood on Leon's breath, she immediately called Brother Ortell to ask what she should do. She was surprised when he said he did not know and that she would be able to take care of him.

Laurine said a prayer and put Leon to bed, put ice on his stomach, and blended his food as one would an infant's meal. They visited Dr. Allred to get vitamin B-12 shots. It took about ten days for Leon to recover enough to go back to his work in Murray. The lower stress of the shoe store was probably good for Leon's health, although Laurine assumed her husband, like any other attorney, would have to grow into his professional responsibilities and would if given the chance. She felt a mild resentment over the fact that he was being held back.

Truth be told, Laurine would have liked to move away from the coal yard, feeling they had done their duty there and could make a greater contribution to the Co-op in their chosen fields. The coal yard was unsafe for children because it fronted a busy road where there were no fences. There was a railroad track to one side and a garage with heavy equipment in the back. Across the street was a wrecking yard that burned old tires. When Laurine put clothes out to dry, they acquired black streaks from smoke and dust.

Sister Vesta used to stop by to see Laurine and attend "mothers meetings." She was revered as the group's matriarch, the first wife of Charles Kingston, whose wise stories about raising children and other topics of interest to the women were highly prized. Laurine's house was convenient for Vesta, who visited a naturopath, Dr. Alfred Smurthwaite, nearby. Vesta had breast cancer and was trying a natural remedy for it. One day she said she regretted she had not taught her sons, Elden, Merlin, and Ortell, how to be graceful losers. They were all overly competitive and stubborn, she said, just as their father had been. Vesta told the women she had never accepted polygamy and that, to keep peace in the family, Charles had taken his second wife as far away as he could get from Bountiful and set up house at the coal mine rather than put up with Vesta's disapproval in Bountiful.

During this period of their lives, Leon thinks Laurine was the strong one who did not let upsets along the way interfere with her overall happiness. She proved herself to be resourceful, loving, compassionate, and flexible, not caring about being praised or receiving recognition. In fact, when the right situation presented itself for her to share her husband with another person, and even though it was a surprise who that person turned out to be, she was just as willing to adjust her world to accommodate a new member of the family as she had been in accepting their call to pull up roots in the avenues and move to the coal yard. She had learned to get by through improvising, both at home and at work, and would figure out a way to accept this new wrinkle in her life as well.

Rowenna

One day Brother Charles stopped by to tell Laurine that her husband would be expected to take another wife because, as a Kingston, he had to set an example. In addition, the family was responsible for preserving the principle of polygamy on the earth. The Co-op derived its power and protection from obedience to that principle. Laurine did not think much about this at the time, but she began to notice that Leon was quieter and more withdrawn than usual, as if he had something on his mind. She wondered if he was being pressured to court another woman. She prayed to know what to do and surprisingly found that she was blessed with a calm, peaceful feeling whenever she thought about her husband taking a second wife.

While at dinner at her parents' home once a week, she saw Leon talking and laughing with her younger sister Rowenna, around whom Leon seemed to feel comfortable. It struck Laurine that Leon and Rowenna were a lot alike. Laurine liked to get things done right now, while her husband and sister were easy going and never rushed. Laurine was anxious about being on time, and her sister and husband were often late. Laurine wanted things done the proper way, whereas Leon and Rowenna did not mind taking shortcuts or breaking the rules from time to time.

Laurine knew that children of plural wives were not always told who their father was in order to prevent them from betraying the secret to outsiders. A child who became too curious about the issue might be severely disciplined. Sometimes the men were afraid to visit their wives before the children were put to bed. Laurine wondered if there were some secret at play that she was not privy to. Sometimes Brother Ortell asked members in private to do something to test their allegiance, which he did not really want them to do. All he wanted to know was that they would be willing to obey him. Once Hyrum Peterson responded to Brother Ortell by saying, "Well, I'll be derned! If I'd a knowed it was a test, I would a done better." Laurine thought about it and decided that this was not a test. It was for real. She took a chance in broaching the topic with Leon and told him she thought God wanted him to marry Rowenna. He responded that he had come to the same conclusion.

When Laurine got married without a wedding cake, she committed herself to learning how to make a cake as a gift to younger women in the Co-op. After learning how to bake and extravagantly decorate a cake, and after receiving a blue ribbon at the county fair, Laurine began taking orders for Co-op weddings. She liked to modify the color and design of each cake to match the couple's personalities. For Rowenna, she chose a sky-blue, three-tiered cake with blue-icing bows to match Rowenna's dress. The year was 1960 and Rowenna was twenty years old—eight years younger than Laurine. The wedding was held in the privacy of the couple's home, as Co-op weddings were. However, when the elders who were to perform the secret ceremony arrived, they determined that something felt wrong and canceled the wedding. They urged the couple to think it over for a few days. Three days and another cake later, the brethren returned and performed the ceremony. Laurine noticed that the Co-op's leaders frequently delayed weddings by saying they did not feel right about it, which she thought was an unwarranted imposition, that whatever spiritual confirmation was needed should have been received at some point before the event and not allowed to disrupt it. It was confusing for everyone involved. Weddings were always performed in the evenings to help camouflage the participants as they arrived and left for the event.

Rowenna changed her name to Erickson to indicate a break from her past but to keep it enough like Ekstrom to be suggestive of her parents' name. The made-up surname was supposed to throw law enforcement off her husband's track, but it proved to be a metaphor for her life over the next few years as she came to question where she belonged. For the first time in her life, she felt like she was filled with confusion, as well as with heartache and loneliness. It was not until she held her first child in her arms that she found something to live for again. She would have eight children, three of whom would follow Laurine's example and graduate from college.

Rowenna moved in with Leon and Laurine at the coal yard until, a few years later, the three adults and their children moved nineteen blocks west to Redwood Road. In the 1970s, the family would experience an even bigger move when Rowenna was placed in a Co-op-owned house in Swede Town to the northwest of the city. All three of these houses were in mixed industrial/residential areas that most people would drive past and not notice, which seemed to be the point. Swede Town was in the middle of an oil refinery and a good place to hide. It was not the ideal street to raise a family on. The problem was that the Redwood Road home had become too small for two wives and twelve children. Once Rowenna had relocated, Leon struggled with how to interact with their children and would stop by for dinner and stay till morning, but not interact with the children beyond a little forced conversation for fear they might suspect he was their father. It was an awkward balancing act. As Rowenna describes it, he was there for the children when they needed to be disciplined but not when they needed to be hugged.

Leon and Laurine would later feel that they missed Rowenna so much, they could not stand to be without her. They therefore built a separate house for her behind their Redwood Road residence, where Rowenna was happy to move in and live to the present. The house was designed to be a generous size, much bigger than Laurine's. When children come to visit today, they stay at Rowenna's house because she has more room, and the nearby adult children who stop in on Sundays for family dinners call Rowenna's home the "party house" because that's where family events are held. Leon and Laurine maintain the house by paying the property taxes, insurance, and utilities, all over the objection of the Co-op. If it were up to the Co-op, there would be more people in the house; but more to the point, Rowenna was subsequently shunned by the Co-op when she developed a love-hate relationship with the leadership and offered her house as a refuge for women escaping abusive fundamentalist marriages.

Laurine's parents

As Laurine's father, Ernie, got older, he felt lonely for his siblings in Illinois. He thought about who had died and who was still left in the Co-op and realized that he did not have any close friends left, which sent him into a depres-

Rowenna married Leon in 1960 and had eight children. Her forceful personality and commitment to social justice were tempered by an element of fun she brought to the marriage, according to Laurine.

sion. This culminated in a suicide attempt. In his day, doctors had little understanding of depression, the doctor at the hospital prescribing Ernie sleeping pills, which he almost immediately overdosed on. Laurine called Brother Ortell for advice and was shocked to be told not to bother him. When another doctor prescribed valium, that helped Ernie somewhat.

Meanwhile, Blenda was nearly blind but was still working at a Co-op dress factory called Valanne's near St. Mark's Hospital. The factory where she worked produced dresses for retail stores, which were marketed to the retailers by sales representatives. The joke at the factory was that with Blenda's cataracts, another woman's bad hip, and other maladies, the dresses were sewn by the lame, the halt, and the blind. In fact, Blenda was desperate to save her eyesight and went on a grape juice fast, which she thought would cure her. This reflected the co-op's prejudice against consulting medical doctors, which was considered a sign of weakness and unbelief. When Blenda's sight did not improve, she finally agreed to have the cataracts removed surgically. Not long afterward, she suffered a stroke and began to lapse into dementia. She died at Laurine's home on May 20, 1983.

Ernie became depressed again. He had already become disillusioned with the Co-op and started working more on the outside and keeping his distance from the Co-op's leaders. In 1987 he had a premonition that he was going to die when he developed extreme pain in his stomach and was taken to the hospital. Laurine stayed with him while he awaited surgery for what the doctors thought was probably a gall bladder problem. At one point, Ernie looked up into a corner of the room and said "Mother." Laurine said, "Yours or mine?" He did not reply. When he went into surgery, that was the last time Laurine saw him alive. His gall bladder proved to be fine, but he had an advanced liver problem. Laurine left the hospital to attend to a breech birth, and when she returned, the surgeon, who knew she was a nurse, let her into the back. She found that the surgery had gone well but that her father had died between the surgical suite and the Intensive Care Unit. An autopsy revealed the liver problem. Laurine delivered the eulogy for her father, as she had for her mother, at a memorial service held in their home. The body was prepared by the same mortuary in Bountiful that had prepared her mother. Laurine's parents were placed alongside each other in the Bountiful City Cemetery.

Pushing back

Laurine had begun acting as a midwife, sometimes visiting women at their homes and sometimes inviting the women to come to her house. One woman she assisted early on, Margaret, seemed to be in a trance for a moment while she sat in a bathtub preparing for the delivery. Laurine wrote on her chart, "Where are you?" but would later appreciate that during birth, women received a sense of entering another dimension, of even teetering on the edge of death as a profound spiritual experience. Laurine read a book by Ida Mae Gaskins, *Spiritual Midwifery,* that she related to. The author was critical of obstetricians who made birth a "knock out, drag out" contest, even pulling the baby out with forceps in the absence of contractions. Birth, Laurine came to believe, should be experienced more fully with the mother's full consciousness rather than less so with the mother being barely present through the overuse of drugs.

With another mother, Laura, there was a different kind of detachment whereby the mother did not seem to care what was happening. The inexperienced midwife was unaware at the time, but would realize later, that her client was experiencing flashbacks to sexual abuse. Society did not know what flashbacks were, and sexual abuse was more prevalent than Laurine would have imagined. One day Laura called to say she was going to kill herself. Laurine told her to put her five children in the family van and drive to Laurine's home. After the client arrived, she could not yet tell Laurine what was troubling her, so Laurine turned to Rowenna, who had recently become certified as a hypnotherapist. When Rowenna hypnotized Laura, she learned the truth of the sexual violence that haunted the woman, and it was the beginning of a long collaboration between Laurine and Rowenna in helping fundamentalist women in need of protection—not that sexual abuse was particular to polygamy but because polygamous women had nowhere to turn when they were abused.

The incident caused Rowenna to become an outspoken critic of the moral lapses occurring within polygamy. Fundamentalists saw her activism as a betrayal of trust, but she saw it as an opportunity her polygamous status gave her to be a spokeswoman for the abused. She founded, with Vicky Prunty, an organization called Tapestry against Polygamy, through which they assembled threads of women's stories about living in plural marriage. To produce a tapestry, they said, you need different kinds of threads and weaves. They chastised fundamentalists for not promoting healthy partnerships between men and women and criticized the State of Utah for taking a hands-off approach to polygamy, thereby enabling the dehumanization of young girls by older men. It was an issue of children being brutalized, they said, not of polygamy per se.

In May 1991, Rowenna outlined several objections to Co-op policies in a letter to Brother Ortell's prominent sister, Ardous, claiming the Co-op had abused her parents and brothers and that the teaching that everyone must obey the leaders or be punished was insidious. As a result of the letter, she was excommunicated from the Co-op on April 1, 1992. Ortell had died five years earlier and his son Paul had assumed leadership of the Co-op. He called in Leon to explain what he thought Rowenna was doing. Laurine waited in the hallway as Leon answered questions before the Co-op board of directors. She had accompanied her husband for the sake of moral support, but since she was there, Brother Paul asked her to also testify before the board. Paul asked her about Rowenna's activities, and she replied that she felt embarrassed by the public disclosure of their relationship, as if she were being disrobed in public.

The board talked it over and decided that Leon and Laurine needed to divorce Rowenna. This was a shock to them—something they could not imagine doing. They had taken solemn marriage vows with her. She was Leon's wife and Laurine's sister, and Rowenna's children were Leon's—nieces and nephews of Laurine. Rowenna may have come to the point in her life that she was opposed to polygamy, but she was nevertheless still participating in a polygamous relationship. Her position was that she had been living in the shadows at the expense of her good health, that her ulcerated colitis was the result of what Virgil Hayes explained in his writings on hypnotherapy came from living a lie. Often our physical discomfort had a psychological origin, according to Hayes. Good psychological health came from being open and frank about one's feelings, beliefs, and activities. Rowenna was not trying to destroy the Co-op, she was trying to improve the quality of her own life.

A compromise was reached so that Leon and Laurine could remain in contact with Rowenna but were banned from attending Sunday services. They were, in effect, excommunicated but were told they could still attend weddings and dinners, which was the equivalent of telling an LDS couple they could no longer attend the temple but could bring a casserole to a ward dinner if they wanted to. Leon was allowed to continue working at a Co-op business, and they were told they could give their earnings to the Co-op, if they chose, which he and Laurine have continued to do to the present. With that understanding, things more or less returned to normal except for the pain they felt over being excluded from the Church they love. In 1994, Rowenna took things a step farther when she called her husband, sister-wife, and her adult children to her house and dropped the bombshell of announcing, without forewarning, that she would no longer live as a plural wife with Leon. She would not break off her friendship with him or her association with her extended family, but in an emotional speech she said that Leon and she would no longer be in a plural relationship, *per se.* It was her own form of excommunication, paralleling the arrangement Leon and Laurine had negotiated with Brother Paul, imposed on Leon and her sister-wife. From that time on, Leon would no longer stop by to see Rowenna in the evenings. However, even now Rowenna sometimes still spends time in Laurine's house. When the family gets together, they mingle easily and have a good time, although careful to avoid certain topics.

The branding of the family as apostates confirmed what many people in the Co-op already suspected about the Ekstroms due to Ernie's longstanding ambivalence about polygamy and, more recently, Laurine's and Leon's pursuit of higher education and professional careers. The family was too close to the center of things to be easily dismissed; Laurine provided a needed service for fundamentalist mothers and Leon's legal background could prove to be a problem if he became an antagonist. They could not be lightly cast aside, in other words. And from the perspective of the Co-op, the family was not really a threat because Rowenna's criticisms, coming from a plural wife who stood up in public and spoke her mind but had not entirely disavowed her plural association, made the Co-op look better than it otherwise might have.

The dynamics of polygamy

As one might imagine—even for those who have not seen *Big Love*—polygamy involves a delicate balance of family interests. The first wife has to accommodate the second while retaining managerial status in the home. The second wife, who is usually younger, has to be sensitive to the disruption she is causing in the relationship of the other two. It only works well if everyone is aware of the others' feelings and behaves gently and speaks softly in all of their interactions. The exception to the rule was Rowenna, whose strength was that she spoke her mind without compromise. It was in her nature to be a dominant personality and insist on things being done according to her preferences. "She does not stamp her feet," Laurine explains, "but she argues her case and doesn't mind if she takes more than she is willing to give in a negotiated settlement." It did not matter whether the discussion was about the use of the kitchen or division of funds or raising children, Rowenna did not begin with the expectation that it would end in compromise. She had the effect of holding up a mirror to Leon and Laurine and forcing them to re-think assumptions about their lives. The sister-wife was not necessarily right or wrong, but she was opinionated. However, where some people imagine polygamy to involve endless romance and sexual bliss, the reality was somewhat different even though the protagonists of this story felt like they were a model family, never raising their voices in anger. They felt that they lived better than the average polygamists because of how well they got along.

Rowenna came to see that polygamy was designed for men, that it was an unhealthy addiction. It was not something they could easily refuse. Laurine agreed, more or less, with that analysis. An odd thought entered Laurine's mind at the last Co-op Church meeting she attended when the words "grandest tiger in the jungle" entered her consciousness, as the men stood and talked about their accomplishments and how many descendants they had. The words Laurine thought of were from *Little Black Sambo,* "which of course we do not read anymore," she quickly added. Once upon a time, she did read this notorious children's book and now remembered the tigers chasing their tails until they turned into butter. Like in the story, men in the Co-op liked to show off their wives and count their grandchildren, she decided. Within the Co-op, it was possible, through Skinnerian means, to control men by allowing or limiting their access to women. In that kind of system, women were devalued and boundaries became blurred. If a man had ten wives and was courting five others, it was not easy to remember the acceptable behavior in each situation, whether one was with a wife or potential wife, with an adult woman or a younger woman.

As the Kingstons came to believe that they were descendants of Jesus, they concluded that they needed to marry within the family to keep the bloodline pure. Increasingly, the men have appeared in court, and in the newspapers, for marrying and conceiving children with half-sisters, nieces, and cousins, indicating that once a taboo has been broken, others come within reach. This is the legacy of early Utah interpretations of biblical precedent. Laurine has been happy to see changes come to fundamentalism, including the way children are raised. Often the purpose of discipline within polygamist families was to break a child's will. Adults used to apply the "Apache death grip" when a child disobeyed, placing a hand over the child's mouth and nose so it could not breathe. Such children grew up without a strong sense of individuality. Although in Laurine's household, the parents disagreed on which approach to child rearing and other domestic controversies would be the best, they met to discuss these things and tried to come to a unified decision. At times, Leon acted as a judge, listening to contrasting opinions, but his decisions often went unheeded. Other times his wives would try to force his hand, but he would become withdrawn rather than stand up to them. They experimented with different approaches, putting various ideas to the test, and if an idea did not work, they would try something else. They were never as draconian as some of the others in the Kingston family, and they may not have always had a clear idea of what the end result should be, but the children always knew that they were loved and that, like in Ernie and Blenda's home, their opinions were valued.

Laurine would not have been able to pursue a career as a midwife without Rowenna's support. The younger sister took care of the children while Laurine attended to births. This was most convenient when they lived together, but other dynamics continued after Rowenna moved to Swede Town. The move may have been necessitated by the sheer number of children in the marriage. With fourteen people and one bathroom, the house was crowded. Brother Ortell gave Leon the option to place Rowenna and her children elsewhere. Even so, it was a difficult separation. Leon had to learn to be conscientious about dividing his time equally and to spend as many nights with Rowenna as with Laurine. In fact, they made a schedule and followed it. One of Laurine's clients became suspicious of her midwife's marital arrangements and would drop in at night, unannounced, and ask, "Where is Leon?" Laurine would say he was "helping Rowenna" and leave it at that. The move was hard on everyone in

the family, especially the children, who had gotten used
to each other. It was like a divorce for them. The teenagers especially felt the sting of it. But studies have shown
that where each wife has her own home, the marriage has
the greatest chance of success. Ortell's wife, LaDonna,
insisted that each of her daughters have her own home as
they married. It really depended on each individual's personality. Laurine thinks people bond together better when
they are in the same house. She prefers that arrangement
and was sorry to see Rowenna go.

Sister wives

When Laurine left the hospital, she worked in private
nursing care for a while and then gradually began doing
midwifery. Rowenna entered the marriage during this
transition. Laurine found that there was a lot she liked
about her sister. Rowenna was strong and handy around
the house, and she was relieved that Rowenna did not
physically discipline Laurine's children. In some ways,
Rowenna loved life more than Laurine did and knew how
to reward herself at the end of the day with some relax-
ation. She seemed to enjoy work as much as play. She
loved the children unconditionally. She was stubborn but
principled and respected other people's space. Laurine
admired how her sister would not do anything just to get
along if it did not meet her convictions, whether political,
religious, or personal. Laurine was more likely to compromise to make other people happy and expect everyone

to do likewise. Rowenna was free with money, bringing more toys into the home at Christmas, for instance. She also had a way of bringing fun and excitement to the family's activities.

The two wives had grown up together as sisters, eight years apart, and knew a lot about each other before they agreed to share a husband. In their parents' family, Laurine's birth was followed by two brothers, so she was happy to have a little sister and amused to see how well Rowenna coped at an early age by not letting any boy dominate her. Perhaps Rowenna was ambivalent about marriage. She may not have seen it as necessary to her happiness. This may be why she was conflicted about polygamy. She appeared to outsiders to be mostly negative about the institution, but she fell short of dismissing plural marriage altogether. She felt as if, because she was living it, she had a greater right to comment on it than scholars did. She was unprepared for the almost immediate decline in her fondness for polygamy from the time of her marriage, which put an enormous strain on the relationship between the two sisters.

Laurine had learned to respect other people's beliefs. This helped her tolerate her sister's differences. Outside of the Co-op, Laurine had encountered doctors, nurses, gurus, professors, and pagans and felt she had learned something from each one of them. This did not mean that she took her own beliefs lightly, only that she did not feel the need to proselytize other people or receive their approval. Just like her tolerance of differences in other life philosophies, she was drawn to different personalities. She liked her sister's feistiness even though it was foreign to her own personality. Laurine continued to be committed to polygamy. Her view was that if lived well on earth, polygamy can give those who earn it a special place in heaven. It will be a place so great that a man and his cohorts will be able to create their own worlds after they have ascended to the celestial realms. When she confides this to a confidant, she is enthusiastic in explaining her heartfelt convictions, which in fact derive from mainstream Mormonism. However, like much within the mainstream Church, this view of celestial propagation on the part of elect men and plural wives began to disappear about a century ago and seems destined for the theological graveyard except through its preservation by fundamentalists.

Laurine remembers how her eyes were opened when she started visiting fundamentalists who were not from the Co-op and walked into homes that were comfortably furnished, with happy children who were respectful of their parents but not robots, and modern, well-educated wives in many cases. Most of the men worked in construction and mingled with outsiders, which gave them a more urbane worldview than a lot of the Co-op members had. Some of her clients (about 5 percent) were non-fundamentalist, but their homes were often indistinguishable from some of the non-Co-op fundamentalist families. For some reason, the path the Co-op had chosen was one of monetary self-denial and sexual excess. She was glad she had been able to see the variety of homes and people and realize the breadth of the fundamentalist experience.

A famous anthropologist, Sheila Kitzinger, looked up Laurine when the researcher was in Salt Lake City for a Utah Midwife's Association convention and asked if she could accompany Laurine on a visit to expecting mothers. Laurine picked her up and took her to a home where the women wore long dresses, long sleeves, and high neck lines and did not believe in wearing makeup. Laurine told Dr. Kitzinger it was all for the sake of modesty, but Dr. Kitzinger said no, it was a means of social control on the part of the men. Laurine thought this over and wondered what it meant that she herself always wore pants (slacks) to births. Some of the polygamists commented on it and felt embarrassed for her because of its hint of masculinity. Laurine had convinced herself that she wore pants to be modest while she assumed the acrobatic positions that were necessary while assisting a birth, but now she admitted to herself that she enjoyed the comfort of them and maybe, to a small degree, what they symbolized.

As she became more familiar with the different ways of being a polygamist, she asked one leader how he knew it was right—or rather that his particular interpretation was right. He said he guessed he would not know until he had died and gone to the other side. Laurine decided that if this were the fact, then not everyone should live in polygamy. Still, she was impressed by the homes she

The more Laurine associated with people outside
the Co-op, the more she understood that there
are individuals of all stripes in the world and that
we can learn something from all of them. Still, her
highest loyalty was to the ideological underpin-
nings of the Co-op. She is shown here in 1988 at
the height of her activity as a midwife.

visited. Some of them, she thought, were a little bit of heaven on earth. She was content with her own situation, living with the two people she loved dearly out of everyone on earth, but she admitted that there were personality conflicts, crowded living conditions, and constant interference from the Co-op that prevented her from enjoying life without any dissonance.

Some polygamists live in one house and add onto it as the family grows. In this way, it can become like the famous Winchester House in California that the owner never stopped adding to, ending up with 160 rooms. Whatever the physical arrangement, polygamy has to be worked at continually, Laurine explains. Sometimes one has mentally to reach inside to remember where one's soul resides, regardless of where the body might be and what chaos surrounds the woman during housework or in attending to childbirth. It's a mental exercise that cannot be acquired quickly. Laurine's mother-in-law, Ethel, told her it took ten years before you knew if polygamy had been the right choice. Laurine noticed that when a man had three or more wives, he was more likely to resort to manipulation to control the women. She heard a young man say, "You'd better believe that in this marriage, I'm going to have more fun because now I know how to do it." The implication, from context, was that he was going to train his new wife to be more obedient and subservient. Once Vesta called and asked Laurine how she was doing with her "miserable life," to which Laurine responded that she was okay but had heard that "misery loves company." They laughed. She remembered hearing Paul Kingston say that the more you lived in the Co-op, the more you lived with the devil. Sometimes while he was still learning the ropes, he would say silly things but his aphorisms were received as the wisdom of the ages.

Laurine thought Rowenna was innocent and needed to be sheltered. She was the younger sister, after all. She did not even go on a honeymoon with Leon. She felt, more than Laurine, the burden of having to try to keep her marriage secret. It made her relationship feel immoral and wrong, and she was uncomfortable around Laurine. The marriage violated an incest taboo that the two sisters had to overcome in their heads, which was not easy. Leon became withdrawn, eventually not even communicating with Laurine at all for a while. Laurine lost weight and became depressed. Leon seemed unable to decide what to do, as if he were lost. It is an untenable state of affairs when people in the same house stop interacting with each other and avoid making decisions. Although they tried their best not to let the children notice their difficulties, it was inevitable that the children would pick up hints of the tensions and would suffer to some extent for the lack of spontaneity and joy in the house.

Laurine's oldest son started having night terrors in which he would get a glazed look in his eyes after Laurine rushed to his room in response to his screaming. "Here it comes! Here it comes!" he would say. Laurine took him to

Dr. Allred and to Dr. Smurthwaite for chiropractic therapy. She took him to Val Sundwall, a general practitioner
whose practice included obstetrics. Dr. Sundwall suggested phenobarbital as an anticonvulsant. Sister Vesta
told Laurine Satan had not been able to break Leon and
his two wives apart, so he was making an advance on the
children. Later the family would learn that the boy had a
slow-growing brain tumor, giving him a short-term memory problem, but for now that revelation was still far off in
the future. The best thing, Laurine found, was to hold him
and stroke his back and talk quietly to him until he went
back to sleep. Doctors say there is a genetic proponent to
night terror and that it affects 5 percent of all children; it
can be triggered by stress.

Leon was still not working as an attorney. His uncle
had him spending long hours at Ensign Shoes in Murray, and now Rowenna was assigned to work with him
at thirty-five cents per hour. Laurine was still a surgical
nurse at County Hospital, while her mother took care
of her three children. Laurine had another girl in 1961,
after which Rowenna had her first child, a baby girl, coin-
cidentally on Laurine's birthday. Laurine assisted Rowenna in the delivery. Both births went well; both mothers
remained calm through their deliveries and the babies
proved to be healthy and happy. It became clear that
Rowenna had a different approach to shopping for baby
supplies than Laurine, who would look for bargains while
Rowenna sought out quality. The products Rowenna pur-

chased lasted longer, but even so, it was hard to defend the extra expense. Rowenna spent more in general, whatever shopping she did. Her boldness to pick up more expensive items took Laurine's breath away. Laurine was timid about such things even if she thought the expensive item would be better in the long run.

One of the reasons the family had moved from the coal yard at 3900 South to the Redwood Road neighborhood was that the street outside the coal yard was being widened and the city wanted them to move. Laurine was willing to go wherever Brother Ortell asked them to go, but Rowenna thought they should tell him where they were willing to live. In the end, Brother Ortell had his way when he found a house, aided by Co-op realtor Lamar Jenkins, that looked like no one had cared for it and that no one would notice if it was inhabited or not. Laurine and Leon still live there today. It was built in 1890, was in poor shape but was an attractive historical structure, and it had three acres of property surrounding it. The family that preceded them had unruly children and a pet monkey who together caused significant damage. With help from relatives, Leon, Laurine, and Rowenna were able to make the house livable and move in by August 1964. They all grabbed shovels to clean up after the monkey and sponges to scrub down the walls and floors. Ernie found two assistants, Mack Frandsen and Alfred Grundvig, to help him repair and remodel the house.

When Rowenna had another baby girl in December

At the 2000 wedding of a granddaughter, Laurine stood
with the love of her life, Leon, who exemplified the
values of the Co-op by working selflessly and cheerfully wherever he was needed, forsaking his law career
in the process. Although the Co-op has been led by
his father, uncle, and nephew, he has not received any
special considerations due to his family connections.

1964, Leon's sister Carolyn agreed to help with household work such as the laundry. Laurine was working at the Cottonwood Hospital and doing home births in her spare time. She had become known as "the little red-headed polygamous midwife on Redwood Road" who could turn a breeched baby, which made her in demand not only among Co-op members but among other people seeking natural childbirth. A breech birth (feet-first or some other position rather than head-first) is difficult even for obstetricians, who often opt to remove a baby through Caesarian-section surgery rather than turn a baby around in the uterus.

Laurine and Rowenna were grateful for the fact that their children liked each other as much as the sister-wives liked each other, and supported each other in school and elsewhere. As they grew older, Laurine's children all married within the Co-op, while none of Rowenna's children did. One of Laurine's children, and three of Rowenna's, graduated from college. Even though they are half siblings, they refer to each other as cousins and to their step-mothers as Aunt Rowenna and Aunt Laurine. Something particularly satisfying to Laurine is that her daughters and step-daughters are not only good wives and home-makers but strong, independent women who could take care of themselves if they needed to, with the possible exception of her oldest daughter who might have learned more from Laurine's early, more dependent mode of living than from her more self-actualized later self.

In any case, none of Laurine's or Rowenna's daughters are like the female clerk Laurine encountered one day in the Co-op grocery store. The clerk's face was bruised around her eye and forehead, and when Laurine asked about it, the clerk said it was nothing and, more defensively, that she had deserved it. With pressure from inside and outside the Co-op, that kind of treatment of women is slowly disappearing. Looking at polygamy cross-culturally, it is difficult to know how much abuse might be endemic and how much is dependent on the larger culture. In American society generally, there is more awareness of the possibility of violence and sexual abuse in families. There are horror stories in the newspaper about the treatment of women and children in Muslim countries where polygamy is the norm, but polygamy goes back centuries in Christian countries as well. For instance, Charlemagne had four wives, several concubines, and many illegitimate children. The Anabaptists in sixteenth-century Germany believed, like Mormons, that polygamy was biblical and therefore necessary. There were abuses among the Anabaptists as young girls were forced to marry older men, but there were also parallel examples in the Middle Ages of girls being given or sold to older men for monogamous marriages.

It may have been the difficulties Laurine and Rowenna surmounted in bringing harmony to their own family that prepared them for rescuing unfortunate girls from abusive polygamous relationships. In their own home, there was not abuse but there was tension until they created an environment that was conducive for troubled women in need of a safe house for healing. If given the chance, Laurine would marry the same way again. If given the chance, Rowenna would not. But Rowenna would not give up her children and step-children or her love for Leon and Laurine. Neither woman would give up her lifetime of service to abused girls or help for polygamous mothers in need of assistance in child birth.

References

Burgess-Olson, Vicky. *Family Structure and Dynamics in Early Utah Mormon Families, 1847 to 1885.* Ph.D. diss. Evanston: Northwestern University, 1979.

Burgess-Olson, Vicky. *Sister Saints.* Provo: Brigham Young University Press, 1978.

Erickson, Rowenna. "Monologue: My Escape from Polygamy," *Journal of Law and Family Studies* 2 (2009): 2.

Hale, Brian C. *Modern Polygamy and Mormon Fundamentalism: The Generations after the Manifesto.* Salt Lake City: Kofford Books, 2006.

Solomon, Dorothy Allred. *Predators, Prey and Other Kinfolk: Growing Up in Polygamy.* New York: W. W. Norton & Company, 2003.

4.

MIDWIFERY

A midwife can be an obstetrical assistant or a wise woman who has a sixth sense about things. She may be female or male despite the fact that the terms *midwife, sage-femme* (French, *wise woman*), *doula* (Danish, *earth mother*), and so on traditionally implied women. In some cultures, such as among the Guatemalan Mayans, midwives are also spiritual guides who not only help deliver the child but also predict its future. In most places in the world, throughout history, there have been women who have assisted other women in giving birth. A hundred years ago in the United States, 95 percent of all babies were born at home. Around the world, 70 percent of all deliveries are home-births, according to Marsden Wagner, a representative of the World Health Organization who spoke in Salt Lake City in 1996 at a midwifery conference.

Home births result in fewer deaths than hospital

births, in part because midwives let the hospitals treat complications; but even so, it is worth noting that midwife-assisted births are safe. They are also inexpensive. A midwife charges about $1,000 per birth, including pre- and post-natal visits, while a hospital's charges begin at about $8,000 for the same services. Another advantage to home birth is the avoidance of technology which, although heaven-sent when things go wrong, create an impersonal and intrusive environment in place of a more comfortable family setting. In fact, there are unintended, harmful effects for some medical treatments women can be subjected to in the hospital, including risks associated with over-medication or over-zealous surgical intervention, which tend to balance out the risks associated with home births separated from the life-saving assistance of medical personnel.

As midwives like to explain, in a hospital environment time is money, so a woman who has been in labor too long will need to have the birth artificially induced. Once that is done, one thing can lead to another. For instance, the woman will probably be given an epidural analgesia, by which opiates are injected into the spinal column, eliminating sensation in the lower body. This lessens a woman's ability to control her muscles and means that the doctor will probably have to remove the baby with forceps or a suction cup called a *ventrouse,* if not by Caesarian section. All of these procedures have unusually high rates of occurrence in Utah, according to Dr. Wagner.

From the standpoint of a midwife, the mother should deliver her own baby, with only as much intervention from the midwife as is necessary. Midwives have a saying that "mothers give birth," not health care providers. To a midwife, birth is a natural phenomenon, more like sneezing or some other bodily function than a disorder that requires surgery. They have a high tolerance for extended periods of labor, false starts, and longer recoveries if necessary. They see birth as a peak experience that a mother should fully participate in. As she gives birth, her body produces oxytocin, which creates the strong bond between mother and child. If the mother is overwhelmed by drugs or medical technology, she misses the effects of her body's natural drug. Birth involves pain, but it can be managed more comfortably at home, all things considered. For example, squatting is more comfortable for a birthing mother than sitting upright or lying flat. Lying in a hospital bed is convenient for medical personnel, not for the mother. In studying births cross-culturally, researchers have found that mothers giving birth in natural settings most often kneel or squat to give birth.

There is a formal career track in the United States to becoming a Certified Professional Midwife (CPM) involving a rigorous written exam and an evaluation of the midwife's performance in the field. Tests are administered by the North American Registry of Midwives in about half the states. There are also Certified Nurse Midwives (CNMs) who receive a B.S. degree accredited by the

American College of Nurse Midwives. The CNMs assist obstetricians in the hospital. The University of Utah was one of the first schools in the country to initiate the CNM degree. In addition to these, there are lay midwives, who are uncertified birth assistants. They sometimes refer to themselves by other terms such as Christian birth guides or community midwives. In any case, they resist government regulation of their craft. As an LPN, Laurine was a special case. Although initially it was difficult for her to navigate the dangers of serving the polygamist community, for whom many births are themselves evidence of a crime, eventually she became certified with the state (CM) through the Utah Midwife Association.

Laurine entered midwifery as an assistant to Rulon Allred. Other lay midwives take this route of learning at the hands of an experienced midwife through a multi-year apprenticeship. Those seeking formal training enroll in a university curriculum, and the level of schooling determines whether a midwife will practice in a hospital and rely mostly on modern medicine or practice out of their home (including sometimes a tent, teepee, yurt, or cave) and rely more on herbal antidotes. Some midwives wear gloves and some do not. Traditionalists sometimes accompany the birth with prayers, chants, or aroma therapy. Lay midwives are keen observers of a mother's state of being and derive what information they need from auscultation and various body measurements, which they follow up with nutritional herbs, massage, and good advice, not only for the delivery but for life in general. Auscultation refers to listening to the baby's heart through the uterine wall.

A good midwife makes plans for emergency support if things go wrong. If she can tell during a consultation that a birth will likely involve complications, she often refers the woman to a clinic, hospital, or mental health facility, depending on the need. Midwives also refer women to lactation stations and other resources. They will generally decline to assist in the birth of twins, births to diabetic mothers, premature births, ectopic (fallopian) pregnancies, prolapsed umbilical cords (when the cord precedes the baby), and placenta previa (bleeding). However, if the mother is within the 95 percentile of normalcy, the midwife will provide a safe, harmonious birthing environment that includes accommodation for the woman's husband, parents, and in-laws, who also need attention during the birthing. Midwives know that it is difficult for the baby's grandmother to see her daughter go through birth. If the grandmother's anxiety can be turned into a calming influence, it will be passed along to the nervous mother.

A short history

After World War I, there was a significant increase in hospital deliveries in the United States, and beginning in the 1930s home birth, breastfeeding, and midwifery went into decline. Americans had come to worship science and the so-called "specialist care" provided by doctors,

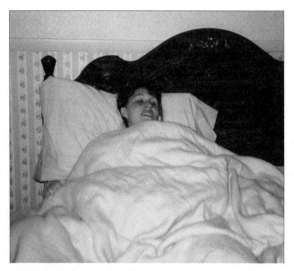

For some women, home birth meant a stay at Laurine's house. Like Blenda and Ernest Ekstrom before them, Laurine and Leon Kingston offered their house to anyone who needed it to give birth and convalesce, as in this instance. It sometimes involved a consideration of privacy for polygamous wives.

most of whom were male. The beginnings of Board Certified Obstetricians emerged, most of whom did not want to
travel to people's homes because it was not cost-effective.
Family doctors continued to perform home births along
with other emergency calls but did not have a lot of time
to devote to it. Obstetricians came to think that their services were indispensable, not just for difficult births but
for normal deliveries, and that women were more or less
incapable of giving birth on their own.

Prior to this development, hospitals were the places
one went to die or nearly die. In that sense, it improved
the hospital's image to include birth in its repertoire.
Health insurance companies proliferated during this time
and preferred the efficiency of hospital staffs, especially in
managing paperwork. This was also the era of a new drug
cocktail called "twilight sleep" (*Dämmerschlaf*), a type of
anesthesia developed in Germany whereby women were
injected during labor with morphine and scopolamine and
the baby was pulled out with forceps. When the mother
recovered, she retained no memory of the birth. Doctors
referred to this procedure as the "knock-out, drag-out"
approach.

Later, intravenous drugs were replaced by "epidurals"
injected into the epidural space in the lower back. As
Grantly Dick-Read, a famous British obstetrician, put
it, epidurals made it possible for a doctor as "magician"
to deliver a baby through "a paralyzed birth canal." Of
course, women don't want to experience pain in birth or

otherwise and are understandably apprehensive about being able to withstand the intensity of it. They enter the hospital afraid that the pain may become so intense, they will regret not having asked for anesthetics. In contrast to this, midwives prepare women for the pain through exercise and mental tasks that are partly designed to help them with their fears. The women are reminded that by giving birth naturally, they protect their baby from the bad effects of the drugs they would otherwise be subjected to. Once a drug is delivered into the mother's system, it affects the baby just as much as the mother. Nor is the drugged woman able to fully participate in the birth process, which is less than ideal. If she can report on and interpret the pain, her feedback is important to the midwife.

A naturally occurring morphine-like substance, beta-endorphin, saturates the mother's and baby's bodies during labor and delivery. With oxytocin, it helps create a euphoric peak experience that at least momentarily overcomes the pain of childbirth and is enjoyable. Christiane Northrup, an MD who writes about women's health issues, calls this feeling one of "joy, love, and ecstasy." The feeling is abbreviated in the hospital experience where everything is hurried up, the sensations masked by pain relievers, and a woman only spends, on average, two hours and fifteen minutes with the obstetrician, including pre- and post-natal care, according to the Wasatch Childbirth Educators Association.

One argument people give for hospital birth is cleanliness, but despite appearances, homes are generally more germ-free than hospitals. Sick people bring a constant infusion of fresh pathogens into the hospital, whereas at home, the fetus is already accustomed to the germs the mother encounters there. According to a 2011 *American Association of Retired People Bulletin*, there are about 100,000 deaths each year in the United States from infections that are contracted in hospitals. Who would want to have a baby there? Especially since a hospital room is less comfortably appointed than a living room or bedroom. Through the 1950s, hospital birth became even less comfortable when fetal monitoring machines were introduced like something out of a futuristic horror movie. The laboring women were strapped to the fetal monitors, making their labor even more unpleasant. A survey in Britain in the early 1980s showed that many of these machines did not work properly anyway, but doctors loved them. For the mother, it wreaks havoc with her ability to bond with the emerging child.

Midwifery in Utah

There have been famous midwives in Utah history. Many people know of Patty Sessions, for instance, who traveled long distances to help women deliver a total of 3,977 babies. In pioneer times, the midwives knew more about birth than doctors, who often lacked proper training, and the midwives were more trusted in any case.

Patty's low opinion of doctors is well-known, as is the support she enjoyed from Mormon leader Brigham Young, who thought it made perfect sense that women should assist women in childbirth. For a similar reason, he promoted the training of female obstetricians in the 1870s. Eliza Snow, one of Young's plural wives, said at a meeting of the Women's Retrenchment Society that women should become doctors in order to keep men out of delivery rooms.

The first Utah woman to earn a medical degree was Romania Pratt. In the fall of 1874, she traveled to Philadelphia and entered the Women's Medical College (WMC) of Pennsylvania. Founded in 1850, it was the oldest and most prominent college in the country to offer M.D. degrees to women. Another Utah woman, Ellis Reynolds Shipp, enrolled in the same college in 1876. As a polygamist, she enjoyed the support of three sister-wives who raised her children while she was away. She gave birth to her sixth child in 1877 in Pennsylvania, where she hired the landlady to look after her baby while she completed a residency at a nearby hospital. Dr. Shipp would eventually have ten children, so her obstetrical work was enhanced by her own experience.

Ellis's sister-wife Margaret ("Maggie") enrolled in WMC in 1875 but soon returned due to homesickness. Upon Ellis's graduation and return to Utah, Maggie found the determination to go back east and re-enter the college, earning her medical degree in 1883. In Salt

Lake City, Dr. Ellis Shipp opened a School of Obstetrics and Nursing in the fall of 1878 to raise up an army of midwives, as she said, to provide for birthing mothers in every Utah community. By 1893, one hundred graduates had been certified for obstetrical work. The Utah State Board of Registration licensed a total of 467 midwives between then and 1906, leaving no doubt as to the thriving demand for their services.

From 1877 to 1881, Dr. Ellen Brooke Ferguson practiced medicine in Utah and taught classes to "ladies" in anatomy, physiology, obstetrics, puerperal disease (infection relating to the placenta), and diseases of children. She was a suffragist and defender of polygamy, which she believed gave women with the aptitude for a career the opportunity to work outside the home. While one woman went to school or worked, a sister-wife could care for her children while another did the housework, each one performing tasks according to her interests and abilities.

Male physicians were getting as much schooling and experience as the female doctors by 1920 but did not immediately replace midwives. They either worked as general practitioners and left birthing to the women or specialized in fields unrelated to reproduction. Dr. Shipp continued to teach her obstetrical course through the 1930s, although a circular issued in 1927 indicates that her school shifted its emphasis to nursing. This was a reflection of the advancing medical professionalism in Utah, which nearly squeezed midwives out of the picture.

Obstetrics as a field of specialty was offered to men in the 1930s, and over time they began to take over the discipline. There was a growing sense in the twentieth century that women belonged at home and that men should be the wage earners in the family. This was a concept that had not previously prevailed in America as an explicit expectation where colonial women had helped run the shops and taverns and do the farm chores alongside the men. Even at home the women ran cottage industries, manufacturing sausages, candles, clothing, and soap and running such errands as taking grain to be milled.

The resurgence of home birth in the late 1960s came by way of the hippy, natural food, and anti-industrial trends of the day. One of its Utah advocates was David Warden, an army flight surgeon who had been to Vietnam and was now the base surgeon at Fort Douglas, overlooking Salt Lake City, as well as being a member of a Mormon bishopric. His wife, Mary Lou, a nurse, was equally enthusiastic in promoting natural birth. They answered people's questions about technical issues surrounding home birth; for this, they were often denigrated by other physicians, and David had the impression that some opposition came from the Mormon Church, which took advice from prominent members who were physicians and were advocating modern medical practices. The Church was concerned about appearing backward or odd in promoting anything outside of the mainstream of American life.

In 1974 at a seminar on home birth in California,

Dr. Warden and his wife met Ronna Hand, who herself had years of experience in home birth and had worked as a midwife apprentice to a physician whose specialty was high-risk pregnancies. She was a Latter-day Saint, so he encouraged her to come to Utah. After being in the state a short while, Ronna was surprised to discover how much hostility she encountered from physicians opposed to midwifery. She nevertheless organized the Domiciliary Midwives of Utah to train midwives and childbirth educators. Home-birth folks comprised an odd coupling of hippies, polygamists, progressives, and Old World traditionalists, all of whom found their way to her Birthing Center in Kaysville after its inauguration in May 1980. Laurine joined the Domiciliary Midwives and sat in on some of Ronna's classes and even tried unsuccessfully to learn Spanish; she offered her help as a midwife for some of the births at the center. She enjoyed the home-like atmosphere of the center and the support from a handful of physicians who would step in when nurse- and lay-midwives encountered complications. The center also energized the opposition by obstetricians, who insisted that home birth was foolhardy and counter-cultural. Home birth had done an about-face since the days of Brigham Young.

In spite of this opposition, the home-birth movement became increasingly popular. Even at the start in Utah, at the first meeting Warden and Hand organized, about a thousand people attended. By 1997 the Associated Press could report a thawing in the initial chilly reception obstetricians had given to midwives, who that year had assisted in some 200,000 hospital births, in addition to helping a growing number of mothers deliver at home. Nearby New Mexico, due to its culture and encouragement by the state, had the highest number of home births in the country, 20 percent.

The legal fight

In 1981 the Utah State Legislature entertained an attachment to a bill making home births illegal. The support for this bill waned after opponents asked the legislators who had been born at home to stand. The majority of older members stood. The legislature decided to create a committee to investigate the matter, and that was the end of the issue for the time being. Another effort was made in 2005 to ban home birth, but proponents of natural birth rallied support and saw House Bill 25 pass, legalizing lay midwifery and making it easier to give birth at home. It seemed that whenever attacked, the midwives gained ground rather than losing any.

The new law established education and training requirements for midwives and listed medicines they could administer. For example, the Rho(D) shot, which is used when the mother's blood type is Rh negative and the father's is Rh positive, was allowed. Oxytocin, which increases the intensity of uterine contractions during a slow birth, was put on the list of medications a lay midwife can administer. It was illegal in the past for them to use any synthetic drugs or even forceps—not that they were eager to use either. Most of them are, to various degrees, opposed to artificial ways of controlling birth and many have resisted the certification that is required to administer RhoGAM, Pitocin, or other manufactured drugs. In that sense, they are in agreement with the Utah Medical Association (UMA) efforts to modify the Direct-Entry Midwife Act of 2005 to keep high-risk births away from midwives. By "direct-entry," the act refers to midwives who enter the profession without formal medical training, directly from the general population.

Despite some continuing opposition from obstetricians, Utah now sees about 600 home births each year, according to the state Office of Vital Records. This means the state has twice the national average, even without estimating the number of births that escape detection by Vital Records. It means that home birth remains an attractive alternative for healthy, low-risk women. For their part, lay midwives remain renegades in some ways, resisting bureaucratization and coming into conflict with nurse midwives, who resent the lay practice of medicine without having gone through the rigors of a formal education. Occasionally the state has prosecuted midwives for the unauthorized use of drugs. In 2000, Elizabeth Camp-Smith, a St. George midwife, was charged for administering Pitocin, though a plea bargain reduced the charges from felonies to misdemeanors.

Not all midwives are as competent or careful as Kingston. In March 2012, two certified midwives had their licenses suspended in Idaho when three babies died at their clinic. In two instances, the women had delayed calling for help. Laurine feels that a birth assistant should be careful not to "wait until the last minute before seeking medical assistance. Doctors make mistakes too and are disciplined for it. Midwives should be held accountable, according to their level of proficiency." Laurine is quick to point out that "midwifery is by nature amateurish" and "not the same thing as the practice of medicine." "Birth is natural," she explains. "It is an individual's right to give birth at home, assisted by the father and a midwife. This is simple and preferable to treating birth as a surgical procedure." Where midwives and doctors are able to work together or in tandem, it produces a good result. When not, tragedy can occur. The real problem, though, may be that in Idaho there was already tension between the midwives and doctors, which is a shame.

Philosophy

Laurine describes the role of the traditional midwife as that of a dwindling minority. She says her clients, like the midwives themselves, were the "salt of the earth," people who "chose to take responsibility for themselves" rather than turn over their health and safety to a bureaucratic medical establishment. She adds that "birth is 97 percent completely normal," requiring little artificial intervention. Occasionally things go wrong, and "when you have a bad experience, it sticks in your mind and makes you cautious, sometimes overly cautious." Of course, "this can happen to anyone in any profession."

"When I enter someone's home," she continues, "a child will sometimes announce the arrival of what she calls 'the baby doctor.' I say, 'No, I am not a doctor. I am the baby lady.'" In homes where she has helped deliver several babies, the older children know that her presence suggests the imminent arrival of a new member of the family. Laurine sees herself as "a loyal friend" rather than a doctor. She is there to help "clean the house, get the washing done, prepare food, make phone calls, and do whatever it takes to help. I have medical training and have taken classes to prepare for home-birth emergencies, but my list of teachers includes husbands, grandmothers, babies, and even animals."

She has found that she loves "all kinds of people. I look deep into their hearts for whatever needs and potential they have, and that awakens a desire to nurture. It gives me a zest for the adventure of life. The memories I have of people are priceless." She says that if she were creating a woman's body, she would not put reproduction and elimination in the the same area. She would put sensation under one arm pit and reproduction under the other and keep them both separate from elimination, which she would keep between the legs. It seems to her that having sensation, reproduction, and elimination all together in one area confuses the mind. There is no sexual sensation associated with pregnancy and childbirth. If reproduction were separate from sensation, then maybe people would make it a more conscious decision to have children. It would also be cleaner and more pure. But in this world, "we have to deal with reality, and it happens to be messier than the ideal we hold in our minds," she says of beatific women blissfully nursing infants in filtered light.

"As I apprentice aspiring midwives," Laurine reports, "I caution them that they should not work so hard that they burn out. It is a demanding practice that requires twenty-four-hour accessibility." The divorce rate among midwives is high. Midwives, she says, are like goats among sheep, and "goats have more personality." The midwife needs to be an entertainer and comforter. She likes to draw analogies between animals and humans, reminding women that animals deliver their babies without any assistance and do just fine. She adds, tongue-in-cheek, that it is a matter of superior intelligence that animals do not need doctors.

Her philosophy includes the traditional concept that the baby is imprinted by the circumstances of its delivery, including who is there and what the atmosphere is like. Those initial impressions leave a blueprint that remains with the individual until death. She also believes that the child is an important, sentient participant in the birth, too often taken for granted at the hospital. Sometimes when she is confused during a prenatal examina-

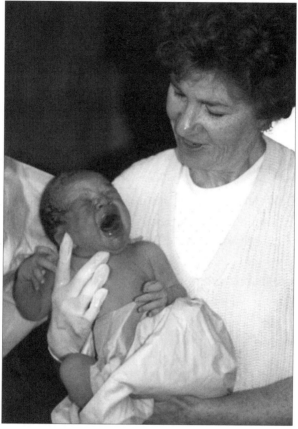

The "baby lady" with a newborn. Laurine understood that
an infant leaving its aquatic environment and learning to
breathe for the first time is in shock. She would whisper in
its ear, reminding it that it was now on stage and needed to
speak the first lines in the drama of its life.

tion or birth, Laurine asks the baby what it is trying to tell her. She thinks the midwife needs to be able to feel the body and the spirit of the baby and considers it a privilege to be present at its birth. In some way, she says, the baby chooses to be born. She draws on an idea taught by Mormon founder Joseph Smith that human beings exist prior to their mortal existence as unembodied spirits which are intelligent and will themselves into the families where they end up. She believes the spirit enters the body at conception but loses its memory of a past existence and matures along with the body.

In order to be up to the challenge of assisting a birth and communing with spirits, Laurine feels she needs to be in good shape physically, spiritually, and mentally. She also needs to recognize the limitations of her abilities and ask for help when needed. She tells apprentices it is not a shame to step back and refuse to assist a birth they do not have a good feeling about or lack the strength to see through. They need to be able to introduce optimism into a home. She asks potential midwives if they can maintain a positive attitude in the face of tragedy, if they can accept God's will over their personal desires, if they can tolerate stress with a clear mind—taking criticism without becoming discouraged and receiving praise in the same modulated way. If not, they might be headed in the wrong direction because midwives come from a tradition that draws on nurturing, spirituality, and healing as epitomized in the work of such pioneers as Hildegard of

Bingen, Maria Montessori, Anne Hutchinson, and Elizabeth Fry, as well as more recent models such as Mary Breckinridge and Jeanne Prentice.

Methods

Laurine considered herself and her clients to be a team, acting in concert as they followed the lessons of experience and of nature to produce a healthy baby. The mother was a thermometer gauge for the condition of the child. The child had needs that were sometimes obvious and sometimes not. The same was true for the mother. Through about 3,000 births, Laurine never lost a mother, nor a baby without first seeking emergency hospital care.

The way she ran her practice, she would begin by interviewing a client to determine whether or not the mother was suitable for home birth. If the woman needed financial help, Laurine would help her obtain it. She would tell a first-time mother she needed to undergo a consultation with an obstetrician and, for moral support, would often accompany the young expecting mother to the hospital as her "birth coach." She would also insist that a young woman receive an overall physical examination and blood work before they proceeded further. The first baby will always be difficult for a mother, not yet knowing what to expect and not yet having experienced the changes her body will go through, after which it becomes easier for her to give birth again.

During the interview with a prospective client, Laurine

would ask why the mother wanted a home birth. In addition to considering the answer, Laurine would watch carefully to study the woman's body language to know how comfortable she was with what was to come. Laurine would ask about the woman's medical history, especially injuries and surgery. It was important to know if the woman was prone to bruise easily or if she had any veins that bothered her. Laurine wanted to know about hormones, the thyroid gland, the general shape of the abdomen, and neurological problems. Allergies were considered, the results of the woman's last gynecological exam or pap smear, and the condition of her teeth, eyes, ears, and nose. Laurine asked how many sore throats the woman got each year, if her skin had changed with the pregnancy, and what her emotional state was.

Sometimes when the husband was in the room, which Laurine encouraged, he would answer for his wife. Later, when Laurine was able to talk to the woman alone, for instance on the phone, she learned that the man wanted a home birth and the woman did not. If the woman answered questions differently on the phone than in front of her husband, this piqued Laurine's interest to dig a little deeper to see whose thoughts were being communicated to her.

She also asked the client to provide a family medical history in areas that midwives know are predictive of a woman's childbirth success, where a mother or sisters might have undergone difficult pregnancies, drawn-out labor, or C-section births. Laurine had young women ask their mothers whether they had taken synthetic estrogen (diethylstilbestrol) after giving birth. Although this was no longer done, it was indicative of a vaginal inflammation or some other problem. Laurine gave each woman a form to take home and fill out regarding birth control and sexual behavior, how they slept, whether they had a cat, and other probing questions. She asked them to think about a designated driver who could take the birthing mother to the hospital if necessary. Laurine asked the women how their family would react if she or her child died within their home. She was amazed by some of the answers, some of which were painfully honest and others remarkably superficial, all contributing to some degree to how Laurine proceeded with the client.

At prenatal visits, Laurine liked to invite the children, husbands, sister-wives, grandmother, and anyone else the mother felt comfortable about having on hand, all of whom were also told they could attend the actual birth if they so desired. Laurine told the children what a special event it was to have a baby. Speaking to the entire family, she would ask about the state of cleanliness of the bathroom, the bathtub especially, because, as she would explain, that is where the mother would need to bathe before and after birth. She would enlist the family members to help clean it, sometimes showing them exactly how to do so. She directed questions to the mother regarding the fetus's movements, its personality, and how she was bonding with it. She checked the mother's blood pressure and listened to the baby's heart tone, also measuring the fetus's growth. She showed the prospective mother how to weigh herself and check for protein and glucose levels in her urine.

A former client took notes on how Laurine led her through the birth of her child, including what occurred during the visits before and after the birth:

1. First visit. I filled out paperwork just like in a doctor's office. She asked me about my:
   a. medical history
   b. birth history
   c. family's/mother's birth history
   d. why I wanted a home birth

2. Second visit. Prenatal examination.
   a. We discussed the first trimester of baby development
   b. She taught me Lamaze breathing techniques

3. Monthly visits.
   a. She would ask if I had noticed any changes to my body, positive or negative. I would get a new assignment to practice for the birth.

4. Semi-monthly. After the thirtieth week since my last normal menstrual period, she wanted me to visit her every other week.

5. Thirty-sixth week. I began visiting her weekly.
   a. She gave me a list of things to procure for the birth

    b. She reviewed the procedure in case I had to be transported to the hospital, what to expect at the hospital, and which hospital we would go to.

6. Fortieth week. She occasionally telephoned and made herself available for calls.
   a. She told me to call as soon as my contractions started, the mucus plug was expelled, or my water broke
   b. She asked for directions to my home and visited me there

7. Labor. Laurine was in and out of the house every few hours, and after I was at about six centimeters she stayed with me.
   a. She organized all of her equipment on a small table in my bedroom
   b. She encouraged me to sit on the exercise ball and move around on it until I felt comfortable
   c. I enjoyed being in the bathtub, so she showed me a technique where with each contraction she poured a pitcher of water over my pubic bone area. This helped to increase the effect and lessen the pain of the contraction.

8. Birth.
   a. After I was at nine centimeters, she encouraged me to find a position I liked and felt comfortable in for pushing
   b. She stayed for an hour after the birth

9. Post-partum care. She came back twenty-four hours later.
   a. She changed the baby's diaper to check the color of the stool
   b. She made sure I had my antibody titer count completed for a RhoGAM shot
   c. She called every twenty-four hours and came back three days post-partum to see if my milk had come in and how the baby was nursing

Recipes

Over the years, Laurine has attended midwife conferences where "we traded and gathered a lot of information." Her training as an LPN prepared her to be able to explain medical concepts to other midwives that they otherwise might have overlooked, along with information about how things are done in hospitals in contrast to traditional methods. As part of her training in a hospital kitchen, she had learned that a healthy pregnancy produces a healthy appetite and that women crave fruit juices and vegetables before and after birth. She also learned how to care for vegan mothers with a variety of foods and sprouts. Not least of all, exercise was also important during pregnancy in order to oxygenate the womb, which is why deep breathing is important. To that end, she encouraged women to walk briskly, swim, and engage in yoga or whatever other exercises appealed to them. A pregnant woman can do almost anything she formerly did, even riding a horse if she wanted to. Getting rid of psychological blocks was important, which is to say that Laurine tried to replace any fearful thoughts a woman harbored with feelings of happy anticipation.

Along with observations and advice, Laurine shared remedies for morning sickness, of which there are as many as there are grandmothers. In fact, each mother has to find what is best for her, but some general principles apply. Everyone agrees that going too long without food is not a good idea, so most women come to learn that eating small amounts of food several times throughout the day works best. Some drink a cup of water infused with lemon juice or apple cider vinegar and a little honey or sugar, cayenne pepper, and ginger. They do so the moment they feel nausea and just enough to feel the warmth of the cayenne and ginger hit their stomach. It helps to know some of these things in advance, and the midwife is a fountain of knowledge about such things.

Laurine knew, for instance, that castor oil helps induce labor. When the cervix is ready and the baby is ready and if the mother wants to encourage it, the baby will usually be born within about four hours after drinking castor oil mixed in a carbonated drink. Laurine would sometimes first "stretch and sweep the cervix" to separate the membranes around the baby from the cervix and to stimulate the area. Then she would send the mother home to mix two tablespoons of castor oil with half a can of soda pop at room temperature, whipping in the oil

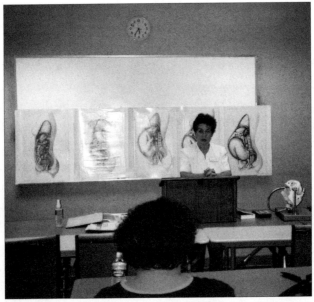

Laurine has given presentations at midwifery conferences, birthing centers, and the University of Utah School of Medicine. She is shown here teaching at Columbia College in Murray, Utah, in 2005.

until it becomes suspended as small droplets, chased by a can of cold soda pop. She would joke that the woman should not go shopping after taking this elixir because the effect could be quick. Two weeks before birth, she liked her clients to take chlorophyll or eight alfalfa tablets a day to help reduce bleeding during the birth. She found that blue cohosh, an herb, helped encourage contractions. She did not use it often but would if the client requested assistance in that area.

Inspiration

Laurine complains that helping women with home births can be a lonely affair without backing from medical people or the general population. The reward comes in the form of spiritual warmth she feels inside. Sometimes she imagines there is a light inside her body. Whatever it is, this feeling of love, warmth, and light is comforting. She treats it as an empirical confirmation of her life's work and of the intuition she receives in specific cases. "Many years ago, I was worried about a girl who was going to have her first baby. I started to think that something was going to go wrong and that I would need to be alert," she said. "I did not sleep well that night. I kept thinking about the young girl." Continuing with the story, Laurine said:

> Driving to Woods Cross to the trailer where she lived, I started crying and thinking, "Why am I doing this? Who

do I think I am? This should be in somebody else's hands." Rationally, I knew I was the best available person at that moment, but I could not feel right about it. Then suddenly something came over me and I was at ease. The sound in the car was hushed. There was a remarkable stillness. My mind became convinced that it was going to be alright, that I should not worry and should just go and do it.

Later that day, the baby was born. Scrutinizing it, I could see that something was wrong. Everyone else said the baby looked fine, but I had them take it to a pediatrician, who diagnosed it with microcephaly, an underdeveloped brain. I felt horrible for the family, but good about the fact that I had done my part as well as I could and that the mother and baby were otherwise healthy and happy.

Laurine considers her intuition to be a sixth sense, born of experience. She has seen enough babies and enough complications that she can tell when something is not right, even if it is unnoticeable to other people. She also believes in acknowledging the miracle of birth, of treating the mother with tenderness, and preparing a safe passageway for the baby. For the latter, she tries to get in touch with the fetus by touching it, visualizing it as she does so. While she does this, she thinks of herself as having a tiny hole in the top of her head that is open to the love and power of the universe and the specific communication the baby's spirit wants to impart.

She further considers it her responsibility to remove anything from her life and mind that would be a psychological block to caring for the mother and child. When

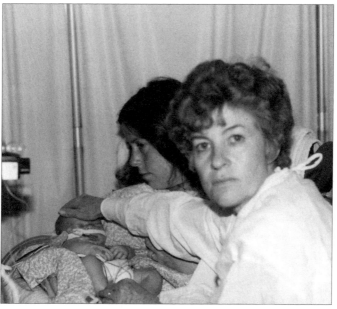

A believer in the importance of touch, Laurine uses the technique to analyze the emotional state of mother and baby. In this instance, the baby was born in the hospital with incomplete internal organs. Laurine stayed by their side to comfort them.

she concentrates on this, she sometimes feels streaks of energy stream from her head into her arms and hands, like an Indian guru activating his chakras, and that this produces a sense that she can heal what she touches. "Sound strange?" she asks. "Try it." She hastens to add that it is not like having a Midas touch but is more of a profound awareness of how sacred life is, that when she is in touch with God, she can bring "healing in her wings," as the Bible says.

She describes her ability to visualize a fetus as a transformation of her sense of touch so that what she feels becomes something like differentiating between various types of "fuzzy caterpillars." "I sense what it is that a person needs and how I can help them. Sometimes I do not have the vocabulary to explain what I feel. I just know that something is needed. Basically, this gift is the ability to see good in everyone and to notice if someone is in pain."

Breech births

Some babies position themselves upside down in the uterus long before birth, while others get turned around at the last minute, in which case the midwife can help by showing the mother how to shift her position in a way that will nudge the baby back into place. Laurine has found that babies are pretty smart about this if given the opportunity to correct the problem. When the baby gets sideways, Laurine tells the mother not to push, to wait until the baby is in position. Then the pushing needs to be connected to the baby's efforts and not in opposition to them. An alert, non-medicated mother can learn how to coordinate her efforts with the baby's movements in the uterus. A midwife can sometimes help untangle the cord from around the baby's neck or relax its hands if it becomes locked around something. She works quickly and calmly, with artistry learned from generations before her. Laurine was warned by an obstetrician that if a breeched baby was born through any other means than cesarean section, the child would end up selling pencils on the street corner for a living. This has not been Laurine's experience even though she would prefer not to have to help deliver a breeched baby.

Pressure points

During labor, the midwife applies pressure against the woman's hips to counter her pushing. If the woman is seated on a chair, and if the midwife pushes on the patella (knee cap), the femur pushes against the hip and counteracts the force of the mother's efforts at pushing. The mother dictates how much pressure to apply. It helps for the husband or coach to support the woman's back. The midwife might also put a pillow at the woman's back. If the woman is on a bed, someone needs to hold her legs while another person applies pressure on her back.

If the woman is standing up, she needs to brace herself with two hands on a wall or some other stable surface. A gentle brush down her back helps to straighten the meridians. The midwife pushes where the woman tells her to do so. Most of the time a flat hand does better than a fist.

Sexual abuse

Laurine learned that women who have been sexually abused present a problem for a midwife because they often hold back and feel embarrassed about being exposed. At first, Laurine could not decipher what the problem was. "I just could not get their babies out," she said. "When it was time to push, the mother was really trying but was only pushing with her face. She could not connect with her perineum," meaning the vaginal area. "If I asked her privately," Laurine said, "it was rare that she had any idea why she could not perform properly." Then she learned that if she covered up the lower region of the woman's body, it made her more comfortable and she was better able to push. "I have been known as the 'cover-up midwife,'" Laurine said. "Other midwives have teased me about it until they try it, then they find that a little security blanket works wonders for some women. I think a blankie makes most of us feel a little more secure," Laurine suggests.

Sometimes she imagines she can feel a cry coming from the fetus, which might be curled up in a tight ball. "Your baby is afraid and does not feel well," Laurine will say to the mother. "Tell me what is going on." After quieting the mother's anxieties, the fetus feels better. If a baby has a traumatic birth, Laurine believes the spirit sometimes goes into shock and stays a short distance away from the body and has to be encouraged to bond with the little body.

A birthing mother who has been sexually abused in the past may have flashbacks to her traumatic experiences. When Laurine senses some kind of emotional conflict, she puts a large blanket around the woman's shoulders and another on her lap and has her sit on the toilet to think about having a bowel movement. She tells her that once the baby is out, she will feel better. She puts a pillow at the woman's back and a support person on either side and then talks about how nice it will be to see the baby, responding to the mother's cues; once the baby comes out, it is amazing to see how healing it can be for the mother.

Some women find it hard to go to the hospital for a birth because they feel vulnerable being around so many men at a time like that. They feel safe and secure at home with a midwife. Laurine adds that as she learns more about sexual abuse, she cannot imagine anything "more destructive to a young, innocent spirit—boy or girl—than this."

Preparation

When Laurine visits a home prior to a birth, after she has inspected the bedroom, bathroom, kitchen, and laundry room, she looks for a way to move the woman out of the house and to the hospital. A long flight of stairs to a basement home is not the best obstacle to have to deal with in an emergency. For the day of the birth, she carries fans and heaters in her car in case it is too hot or too cold. At thirty-two weeks into gestation, she gives the prospective mother a list of things she will need to have ready on the day the baby decides to come into the world:

1 waterproof bucket or waste basket with a plastic bag inside
4 clean towels
6 washcloths
8 firm bed pillows
1 box of 22x30" waterproof underpads
1 waterproof drop-cloth, curtain, or cover for the bed
1 six-quart pan for boiling water
1 box of maternity Kotex pads
1 package of adult diapers
1 bottle of Listerine mouthwash
1 large squeeze bottle (old shampoo bottle)
1 bottle of rubbing alcohol
1 box of Fleets enemas
1 new roll of white toilet paper
1 good flashlight
2 hot water bottles or a heating pad
1 digital thermometer (with a beep)
lots of juice or tea and light food
3 trays of crushed ice

1 box of flexible drinking straws
1 carton of powder or deep-heat rub
1 stick of lip balm
1 short gown
1 blouse
1 pair of slippers or heavy stockings
1 robe
1 camera with film
lots of diapers for a newborn
1 car seat
lots of baby clothes

Laurine asks a woman to have a clean bed made up as soon as she starts her labor and to cover as much of the bed as possible with a waterproof sheet, then to put a normal bottom sheet over the entire bed, tucking it all around and anchoring it with pins if needed. She asks that a woman have two washable blankets nearby and a dresser or table cleared on top for medical equipment.

Breathing

The way we breathe can belie a given physical or emotional state. Conversely, when we are in a state of agitation or stress and force ourselves to breathe in a measured way, we can alter our state of being so that we feel calm and relaxed. During birth, the mother needs to keep a constant supply of oxygen to the uterus, but if she breathes too quickly, she can hyperventilate. It depends on the woman, but if she forgets to breathe in a measured way, the midwife or spouse needs to remind her to keep a slow, relaxed pace. If she does it properly, she can keep the baby oxygenated for a long time without getting out of breath. It helps if she puts her tongue on the roof of her mouth to prevent her throat from getting dry.

It is most difficult to maintain an easy rhythm during contractions. Between pushing, the mother can take shallow panting breaths in a way that feels natural but should return to a measured pace of unnatural breathing when the next contraction occurs. The mother knows when she has overdone it because she will begin to feel dizzy. In that circumstance, she can cup her hands and hold them over her nose and mouth to breath in carbon dioxide or hold her breath for a few seconds when the contraction is over. Laurine smiles at the importance breathing assumes in popular culture, in the portrayals of birth in motion pictures and on television. It is one aspect of birth to be aware of, but not to the exclusion of everything else— even if one were to cynically assume it was a task to keep the husband or birth coach busy when there is actually so much else for them to do that is of equal or greater importance.

Coaching

A coach plays an important role in helping the mother stay relaxed and in guiding her labor by means of two assets: the voice for encouraging the mother and hands to reassure her through gentle touching. If the mother gets too tense, especially during a contraction, the coach should help her relax more during the next contraction to keep the birth progressing evenly. It helps to make physical contact with the mother, even if only by holding her hand. It is equally reassuring for the mother to hear the coach's voice during the contractions. In between, the coach should listen to what the mother has to say, then try to keep her focused on the present rather than on "how long it has been" or "how much longer is it going to be."

If the mother experiences pain in her lower back, it is because the baby has moved lower in the birth canal. The coach can help relieve this pain by applying a deep-heat Mentholatum rub to the mother's back. Even though the mother may want to give up in the middle of a contraction, she needs to bring continuous pressure to bear or it can cause serious interference and delay. During all of this, it is helpful if the coach keeps a loving hand on the mother's shoulder to help her relax her muscles. The body responds to touch and communication.

A sudden change of plans

A midwife needs to know when things have spiraled out of control and the best thing is to get the mother to a hospital. Laurine, for one, never hesitated to implement Plan B, which she had previously reviewed with the mother and asked the father or designated driver to rehearse. She was known for acting quickly if any of the following occurred:

1. A day passes since the rupture of the membranes (breaking water), introducing the possibility of infection to the fetus

2. Prolonged labor or failure to dilate during labor

3. Marked change in fetal heart tones during a contraction

4. Sudden change of fetal activity

5. Heavy blood flow at any stage of birth or postpartum

6. Sudden, unusual abdominal or uterine pain

7. Sudden cessation of uterine contractions

8. Signs of shock in the mother

9. Marked increase, decrease, or fluctuation of the mother's blood pressure or pulse

10. Abnormal presentation of the fetus other than cephalic (head) presentation

11. Prolapsed or tangled umbilical cord

12. Premature labor beyond 2½ weeks out

13. Sudden increase in temperature above 100 degrees Fahrenheit

14. Dehydration

15. Failure to deliver a placenta within two hours

16. Need for vaginal or perineal repair

17. Abnormalities in the infant such as respiratory distress or no sucking reflex

There are reasons that a midwife might be reluctant to rush a woman to the hospital, all of which have to be overcome. The mother, too, faces psychological impediments to giving up on a natural birth and needs to be encouraged. She faces a fear of the unknown, of strange surroundings, and even the possibility of death. Families with limited resources are apprehensive about the costs. There is a sense of losing control over the situation, as well as disappointment, guilt over having made the wrong decision about having a home birth or perhaps being the cause of the problem. "If only I had eaten right, this would not have happened," a mother can think. There is an emotional drain and potential for clinical depression.

The midwife needs to help the mother through these emotions that a dash to the hospital brings. Through the chaos that may ensue, the midwife needs to keep gentle and harmonious control, first calling the hospital to notify the emergency room of the situation and speak to a physician, if possible. She needs to keep her voice calm, state that she is a lay midwife, and state what the problem is, asking for emergency transportation if available. If she is refused transportation or admission to the hospital, as sometimes happens, she should ask what to do.

Both the mother and baby need to be dressed warmly for the ride. The baby should be swaddled in two blankets that have been warmed in the dryer, with a plastic lining or blue pads between them. Before dryers, midwives used to warm the blankets in the oven. The midwife needs to ensure that the baby has a good airway. If oxygen is available, it should be employed. It is important to hold the baby. It too needs reassurance. At the hospital, the midwife keeps in mind that "she is in their house now" and remains appreciative and helpful but not intrusive, keeping her statements informative and brief. She writes down names for future reference. All the while, she has to be careful not to sign anything or give away too much information about herself.

When the mother and child are in good hands, it is time for the midwife to withdraw and undergo her own means for fending off doubts and mood swings that can follow such a disappointment. It is best to talk through the experience with someone who understands it and to analyze what she did so that, if anything could have prevented the turn-about in fate, she can be sure to avoid that path the next time. She will also, of course, call the woman to monitor her progress at the hospital and may make a discreet visit.

Post-partum care

In the 1950s, not everyone had a telephone, so a midwife might call a neighbor to talk to her client. Laurine remembers when she was working in surgery at LDS Hospital and assisting a birthing mother at an impoverished home in Kaysville where it took three days of on-and-off labor for the baby to be born. Laurine called in sick at

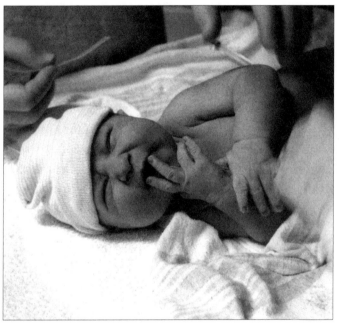

The baby (Victoria's grandson, Robert Saxon Vermaas) was wrapped in two layers of blankets, pinned together with a plastic lining between them, and given a warm hat for his transport to the University of Utah Medical Center in 1997. Laurine was never slow to seek medical help when a problem developed.

the hospital and had to walk a mile to get to a phone. The snow was up to her knees.

She was committed to visiting expectant mothers twenty-four hours before a delivery. When she could not do so, she relied on grandmothers or oldest daughters to fill in for her. Laurine always tried to become accepted as a member of the family by helping with dishes, cooking, and changing the baby's diapers. At first, she did not use gloves and did a lot of hand washing. She asked the mother to wash her anticipated birthing laundry separately from other clothes and dry them in the sun, then wrap them in a large sheet to wait for the birth day.

Laurine would visit a new mother up to ten days after a baby was born. She worked for a doctor who did home deliveries who was glad she had time to "sit at the little ladies' bedsides" because he did not, and before long he had decided he was too busy to continue doing home births. One of the reasons Laurine visited women afterward was to monitor their exercises. She encouraged them to begin doing Kegel exercises immediately after they delivered the placenta. Even if it hurt a little, it was important to regain muscle tone and prevent post-delivery problems. It involves clenching the anal sphincter and related pelvic muscles and was named after a German physician who invented it.

On the second day, Laurine encouraged the women to do a torso stretch, which meant lying on their backs with their knees bent and stretching their hands across their legs toward the opposite thigh. On the third day, she had the women pretend they were holding a candle at arm's length and blow it out with a good spurt of air, contracting the stomach muscles in the process. On the fourth day, the mothers were instructed to do hip rolls, lying on their backs and rolling from side to side while keeping their backs flat. On the fifth day, after the heaviest period of lochial discharge was past, the women were told to do pelvic rocks, which meant dropping to their knees and assuming a wrestler's bottom position, then alternately arching their backs and doing obeisance to an imaginary statue. This further strengthened the abdominal muscles and helped the internal organs re-settle.

Epilogue

Laurine was drawn to the medical profession because she enjoyed working in hospitals, but she preferred the freedom she found on the outside where she could perform her midwife chores without restrictions. As a lay practitioner, she could introduce her patients to the spiritual side of birth and bring intuition and even religious ceremonies to the event. She did not see herself as the center of attention but rather as an instrument of God's purposes. She imagined she was performing in a symphony or opera where the baby might be seen as the composer and the mother the conductor. Laurine's job was to watch for subtle cues from the moving baton, hoping to do her part to bring everything to a smooth conclusion.

She has found it interesting that some families respond to birth as if it is a party, whereas others are filled with dread as the time approaches. In the animal kingdom, births occur by instinct, and they seem to do better when left to themselves. Laurine wonders whether the outcome would be different for human beings if we turned off the machines and let nature take its course, only intervening when necessary. There is nothing, she contends, like the miracle of seeing it all unfold without technology. "How wonderful!" she exclaims and never grows tired of it.

"The most spiritual high I have ever had was at a birth," she continues. "Birth is so complete. You feel at one with the Creator who made the trees, the sky, the water, and air. I have never left a birth without feeling inspired even though I feel physically exhausted." Midwifery involves women helping women by passing on inherited wisdom from their midwife mothers and grandmothers. Two hundred years ago in England, a man was executed for attending a birth. How curious that now most obstetricians are men. Although Laurine welcomes the infusion of men into the birthing room, where they add their own talents to the process, they nevertheless lack the added sensitivity that women acquire by giving birth themselves. Maybe nurse midwives working alongside male obstetricians in a hospital represent a workable compromise, but Laurine still thinks too much is lost, both for mother and baby, by removing them from the home and putting them in an environment that is antiseptic in every way, including spiritually.

The United States has the twenty-sixth lowest infant mortality rate in the world, which means that twenty-five countries have a better record than we do. In those other countries, women tend to give birth at home or at birth centers and not in hospitals. They make extensive use of midwives. They give birth naturally. They breast feed. They are not all as modern, according to our presumption, but they are more likely to understand what a joyous journey pregnancy and birth are.

References

Vicky Burgess-Olson. *Sister Saints*. Provo: Brigham Young University Press, 1978.

Victoria D Burgess. *Home Birth and Midwifery*. Salt Lake City: By the author, 2007.

Christiane Northrup. *Mother-Daughter Wisdom: Creating a Legacy of Physical and Emotional Health*. New York: Bantam Books, 2005.

5.

"I WOULD

NOT HAVE BELIEVED IT"

Real-life Episodes in Midwifery

✳

Typically the mother finds her first experience with birth to be "so exciting!" Laurine says. "The poor baby is a trail blazer, the parents not yet knowing what to do to guide it." Parents are predictable in some ways in that they always hope the second child will be of the opposite sex, and by the third child, they are so used to the routine, and the mother's body is in such great shape for giving birth, that they typically sail through the birth. The fourth time can be a little more difficult because the mother is getting older and the family has to deal with the increased responsibility of a larger family. If they have a fifth baby, they rely on the oldest child to help tend it. By the time they get to the sixth baby, they are in for a difficult time, no matter how you look at it. If there is a seventh baby, the woman's attitude is, "Oh, let's just get it over with." By the eighth birth, the mother survives any way she can with limited emotional resources.

Eighty percent of the babies Laurine has assisted in their birth into the world came from large polygamous families, so she saw the range of expressed and suppressed feelings about adding one more soul to a family. It might be funny if it were not tragic to see women give birth who were emotionally or physically unprepared at that moment in their lives but tried to convince everyone around them that everything was fine. Then again, Laurine had her own large family to care for and understood the mixed feelings one more pregnancy can bring.

An example of differing responses to birth, based on age and circumstances, would be that of Greg and Olivia. Greg had a wife and family already when he met Olivia, and he acknowledged that he was not very good with children. His wife had opted for hospital births and was not interested in adding any more little ones to their litter of five. But Olivia, who was thirty years younger than Greg, turned his thoughts to reproduction. This pretty young woman was not interested in pursuing an education and looked forward to having her own big family. When Greg converted to polygamy, it was partly due to his love for Olivia. He was a successful businessman who could afford to have a second wife. His first wife and children were caught off guard when he confessed his love and newfound theological zeal; nor were they persuaded by his interpretations of dreams, which he said had confirmed that Olivia was heaven-sent. He wanted his family to meet this new love of his. When they did, they were surprised to find that she was mentally challenged. Once they had met her, they thought there was no need to see her again. Greg continued with his plan to add her to his family and procured a separate apartment for her.

Imagine the awkwardness, Laurine recounts, for a midwife to be brought into the middle of a tense family situation. "The important thing is not to judge," she counsels. In this case, Olivia was already pregnant by the time a midwife was brought in. Laurine was shocked at her age, compared to Greg's, and by the fact that Olivia was barely an adult in emotional terms, completely dependent on Greg for everything outside her apartment. Laurine felt sorry for them and agreed to conduct prenatal care at Olivia's apartment.

When it came time for the birth, Greg filled the apartment with flowers, food, and gifts for the mother-to-be. Laurine cannot remember seeing such a display of love and affection. Greg proved to be a good birthing coach. Laurine knew that women who are challenged mentally often do well at birth, and it was true in this case. Two years later, Greg called again for assistance with another pregnancy, this time in a home he had rented in an exclusive east-side neighborhood for the birth. Over time, Laurine would assist the couple through six births, all in different homes in increasingly luxurious locations. Olivia loved all of her children and was a good mother. Greg continued to be indifferent toward children, showing little patience for crying, needy kids, whom he typically put in a room full of toys and told them to entertain themselves. When Laurine last heard from Greg, he and Olivia had joined a group of polygamists in Manti, the True and Living Church of Jesus Christ of Saints of the Last Days. He left his first wife and family behind in Salt Lake City and saw them infrequently after that.

As Laurine tells the story, she describes the ambivalence she felt over the difficult issues it presented to her but says she believes it is not for her to judge. She has always been committed to the dictum of medical ethics whereby a doctor or nurse is expected to offer assistance without regard to a person's legal or moral standing. Complicating the matter, Laurine has always felt pulled in two directions between two different worlds, neither of which acknowledges the authority of the other to make ultimate decisions about marriage, manner of birth, and family life.

Jitters within the family

Laurine grew up quickly at sixteen years old when she was asked by Dr. Allred to help assist her mother, Blenda, through the breech birth of Laurine's baby sister, Sheila. Laurine remembers vividly how hard it was for her to watch her mother suffer. When the baby finally emerged, Dr. Allred placed it on Blenda's stomach where it gasped for breath for at least an hour, as some babies do after an abnormal birth. Thereafter, Laurine tended to her mother and sister as they recovered. She remembers that because she worked so hard to make her mother comfortable, she was herself exhausted at the end of each day.

When Sheila married and had her own babies, Laurine was there again, now to assist her baby sister in childbirth. The first birth went well enough; what stands out in Laurine's mind is the birth of Sheila's second child, which occurred on a cold Groundhog Day when the streets were icy but everything was warm and comfortable inside their parents' house on 900 East in Salt Lake City. If it had not been such hard work, it would have been like a second Christmas in February. A new child can bring a sense of excitement to a house and the feeling that God and nature have blessed the family with a precious gift. This birth was no exception. Laurine also remembers being asked to assist with a sister-in-law's delivery in Bountiful, north of Salt Lake City. By the time she got there, the baby had already been born and her brother Virgil was in shock. The mother was feeling fine and joked that even though the baby was born on the toilet, she was not going to name him John.

Laurine assisted in every one of her sister-wife's births. Being at her side through eight deliveries no doubt helped cement the bond Laurine still shares with her stepchildren, which is almost as strong as what she feels toward her own six children. The intensity of feeling is reciprocated by Rowenna's offspring, one of whom recently sent Laurine a Mother's Day card without either of them thinking it was unusual. Although Laurine defends her decision to help Rowenna with her deliveries, she is glad she drew the line at helping with her own daughters' births after one failed attempt, in the wake of the emotional trauma that can follow.

Things began well enough in 1978 and then quickly deteriorated from bad to worse. Laurine says she should have known the baby's head would be too big to emerge without trouble, but she ignored the warning signs until the head tore open her daughter's perineal membranes, causing semi-permanent damage and excruciating pain. The guilt Laurine felt over not having performed an episiotomy was acute. An episiotomy is where the midwife or doctor cuts open the passageway and sews it back together afterward, leaving little damage because of the clean cut. In the case of this grandchild, the baby then had "meconium aspiration," which means it had inhaled its first bowel movement. More guilt. Laurine called Primary Children's Hospital and learned they were full, so she transported the baby to the University Hospital, which spent five days saving the baby from this life-threatening condition. Laurine even felt bad about this, thinking she was probably misappropriating the Co-op's funds and devoting special attention to her daughter's baby that she might not grant someone else's child.

As they say, time heals everything. Her daughter went

Leon and Laurine with their six beautiful children in 1967. Laurine had recently quit working at Cottonwood Hospital to devote herself full-time to midwifery. Her sister-wife, Rowenna, who herself had eight children, helped run the house.

on to have four more children, the last one in a hospital with the aid of medical insurance and encouragement from Laurine, who could not have been more pleased to know her daughter would be surrounded by emergency medical resources. This meant that Laurine could relax and enjoy the birth like any other grandmother. After all, a hospital was where you wanted a woman who had previously encountered complications, was it not? Wrong!

When her daughter's birth was overdue, the doctor induced labor. Laurine arrived with her daughter and son-in-law at 6:00 a.m. and found the staff to be gracious and helpful, everything routine. A nurse set up a slow Pitocin drip. The monitors were turned on and the atmosphere was quiet and relaxed. Everyone was happy. Two hours later the Pitocin drip was increased. Laurine's daughter was feeling uncomfortable. She was told she could have an epidural anesthesia if she wanted it, and she decided that she did. This was not in defiance of her mother but was the consensus after calmly talking through the options. "Why not!" they thought. The year was 1991. It was a modern age.

Then there was another distraction. They were told that it would take about forty-five minutes for the pain to go away, but forty-five minutes came and went without any relief. They called for help. The anesthesiologist came into the room and checked the epidural pump and stated that everything was fine. The contractions were increasing in intensity. The young technician lectured them and said the mother should not expect to be totally free from pain, that everyone feels pain a little differently. The contractions were getting stronger. Laurine knew something was wrong. She decided to ask Rowenna to come to the hospital to hypnotize her girl.

Rowenna asked Laurine's daughter, under hypnosis, what the matter was, and the mother-to-be answered that her baby was drowning. At that, the nurse turned the birthing mother on her side and found the epidural detached from the mother's back; it had slipped out, dampening the bed. After the anesthesiologist replaced the epidural, the doctor checked in and found, through a sonogram ("ultrasound"), that there had been a placental abruption, meaning that the placenta had separated from the uterus and was causing internal bleeding. A C-section delivery was set up.

Laurine was allowed into surgery and was able to help a new scrub nurse identify some of the instruments she was unfamiliar with. It was 7:20 p.m. when the baby girl was finally lifted from her mother. It had inhaled blood, so its little lungs needed to be suctioned; she was given oxygen and an IV drip and then transferred to Primary Children's Hospital. Her mother was not allowed to see her until the next day. The baby stayed in the hospital for a week and a half.

When Laurine's next-oldest daughter gave birth, it was to a baby that was completely upside-down. A cousin training to be a midwife assisted, which gave Laurine the luxury of being able to focus on the bigger picture and enjoy her grandmotherly emotions. Still, she remembers that the little baby's legs were long and would not immediately stretch out to point downward because *in utero* they had been bent over her head with no room to stretch out. It took three days for the baby's legs to become limber. Whenever Laurine sees her today, now a slender, willowy woman whose legs are still long, she thinks of the difficult birth.

The same mother had a second daughter soon thereafter. As she was walking from the bathroom to the bedroom, she felt like pushing, and in no time, the baby was born in the living room. They were all grateful they had put waterproof pads on one of the chairs in case of emergency. When the father arrived, he was so elated he called his friends and relatives. They immediately came by and filled the house with oohs and awes, lots of food, and too many people for the good of the mother but it was a fun celebration nonetheless.

The next time this daughter had a baby, she followed the lead of her older sister and had it in a hospital. Laurine remembers it well, only partly because it was Christmas Eve and the staff was sparse. The weather outside was a white-out. Like it or not, the baby came when the doctor was still rushing down the hall, no time for an epidural. The mother and baby went home the next day, the baby wearing a little felt stocking on its head. Laurine was liking the trend of her daughters' babies delivering themselves.

One of Laurine's granddaughters with a newborn. Despite Laurine's best efforts, she found she could not be a midwife to her own offspring and eventually settled on being a grandmother in those instances. Ironically, her family has preferred hospital births over assisted home births.

Her third daughter was another story because she had a small, tight pelvis. With a mixed record of Kingston births at the hospital, Laurine decided to try again to see one through at home. Her daughter was in labor for an unusually long time, but finally the baby emerged and was in perfect health, to everyone's relief and encouragement. The girl's second baby was two weeks earlier than expected and was jaundiced or yellow. Laurine called a pediatrician, who admitted the baby to the hospital and treated it with IV fluids and ultraviolet radiation therapy for three days. Although Laurine knew that anything can happen at birth, that it is not the midwife's fault when nature throws a birthing mother a curve, it was nevertheless so traumatic when it involved her own daughters and stepdaughters that it gave her pause. In the end, despite an initial determination not to, she helped birth all but four of her own grandchildren.

Underwater birth

A lot of women are attracted to underwater birth. The impulse for terrestrial beings is to think the baby could drown when it emerges into a bathtub or swimming pool, but the baby is used to a water environment and does just fine if brought out of the water soon enough. Mothers find warm water to be relaxing. Their blood pressure drops when they ease into the bathtub during labor. It minimizes the stress and pain of childbirth. Sometimes the mother catches the baby as it comes out into that environment. For the baby, the transition to the open air is what is difficult. Laurine will bring a baby out of the water and place a towel over it, then pour warm water over the towel to keep the baby warm and ease its acclimation. She tells the mother to encourage the baby to nurse at that point.

Her first attempt at a water birth did not go as smoothly as she wanted. Part of the problem for her was that she had never learned to swim. She only agreed to the procedure because the woman who called her, Karen Breisch, was enthusiastic and insistent. She was a social worker and her husband, Stuart, was an ER physician at one of the local hospitals. They had been studying different types of home birth and became convinced that water birth would be the gentlest for the baby. Stuart had seen enough of chaos and infections at the hospital to doubt whether a hospital birth was superior and liked the idea of bringing their child into a more calming home environment. After all, birth was not a medical event *per se,* he said. If something went wrong, he was a doctor, and they could always drive to the hospital.

Laurine wondered if their medical friends might try to talk them out of a home birth. "They have tried," Stuart said. "Of course, they have seen worst-case scenarios, so they think home birth is too risky." Karen said she was herself certain about home birth and wouldn't be talked out of it. She was a beautiful, strong woman who had once been a guide on the Colorado River. She and "Stu" were soul mates in their advocacy of taking good care of their bodies and nurturing their spirits through outdoor activities.

Laurine confessed that she had never helped deliver a baby in water except in a bathtub and that she would need to learn something about it. They shared with her some literature from France and Russia and a video by Karil Daniels of San Francisco, *Water Baby: Experiences of Water Birth*. Karen was seeing an obstetrician for pre-natal care. The doctor said he would be happy to be on call when Karen approached the end of her term. Laurine visited the house where the baby would be born so they could plan the details. The house was a modern structure and invitingly decorated. She was greeted in the entranceway by an aphorism in a small picture frame: "I welcome you into my home with love and respect." Karen and Stu were thoughtful and gentle. Laurine concluded that it would be a lucky baby that was born into that environment.

The Breisches had decided that the hot tub in the back yard would be suitable for the birth. Laurine was worried when she saw it was on a platform up three wooden flights of stairs but agreed that a June birth in the open air would be nice. The couple was cultivating flowers in the backyard so it would look nice in the background of a video they asked another couple to film to document the birth. This would be a trail-blazer baby in more ways than one. Although it would be Karen's first birth, she was thirty-three years old and inexperienced at this. When the day came that her labor began, she was filled with anticipation. Unfortunately, the labor continued for three days. Laurine finally told her she needed to give up and let them take her to the hospital.

While they deliberated, Karen's water broke, tinged green because of the presence of fecal material. Laurine said that even though they had been thinking about the ocean, aqua marine was not the color they were looking for. They raced to the hospital, Laurine driving behind the parents and baby, bringing the medical records with her. At the hospital, the staff was happy to see their friends; they made sure it was a textbook delivery for the eight-and-a-half-pound baby. "Next time will be easier," Laurine assured the mother.

Three years later, Karen was pregnant again. On a cold April morning, with ice crystals forming on the lower stairs of the hot tub, everyone was in place for a second try at a water birth. Laurine had on a sweat shirt and leg warmers against the cold. The plan was for Stuart to float Karen to the edge of the hot tub where Laurine would assist if she needed to but otherwise allow everything to proceed naturally. Laurine was shivering, so Stuart got her a down coat from the house. With the help of light from the camera, Laurine could see the baby's black hair in the birth canal. The baby was not coming out as planned. Laurine slipped into the water to find the baby's shoulder stuck in the vaginal passage in a condition called shoulder dystocia and the umbilical cord wrapped twice around the baby's neck. Laurine surprised even herself at how quickly her hands worked to move the baby into proper position and untangle the cord.

Before she knew it, Laurine was lifting the baby out of the water and whispering into its ear, "Now you are on planet earth and have to breathe to do what you are here for," at which, thankfully, it breathed. This little pep talk was how Laurine sometimes brought a baby's spirit out of the shock it experiences in birth. When it gasped for breath, she handed it to its mother. "Good thing he had a long cord," she wrote to end her report.

The coat Stuart had given Laurine was saturated with wet feathers; she had to remove the weight of it to get out of the hot tub. As she sloshed down the stairs in her sweat shirt to where a fire was burning in a fireplace, she thought, as she recorded in her report: "I need more practice organizing for water birth. It was really traumatic for me." But on a happier note, "the parents were very happy with their nine pound ten ounce son."

Nineteen months later they were all at the same hot tub for the third attempt, which was "a charm," Laurine remembers. They thought to enclose the hot tub in a tent and put a heater in it to protect against the November chill. Karen had become used to the pregnancy and liked to curve her arm around her belly and talk to her unborn child, saying "My little Kali, we are so close." It turned out to be a perfect water birth. "A bright-eyed, alert, beautiful eight pound twelve ounce baby girl" was the result,

Laurine wrote. "I am still alive and dry. Birth is a miracle in or out of the water."

Laurine had come to love the Breisches and was heart sick to learn, two and a half years later, that Karen had contracted terminal cancer and died. Twelve years after that, Stuart took his three children on a Christmas vacation to Thailand, where they were in a beach bungalow at the Khao Lak Emerald Beach Resort on the morning of December 26 when the tsunami hit the shore, carrying fifteen-year-old Kali out to sea. A few days later, the ocean delivered her dead body back to shore. She was among the 57,000 casualties of that day's tidal waves. Reading about it in the newspaper, Laurine was stunned. "What grief I felt," she said. "Memories flooded over my soul. I knew her! I had assisted her mother in giving her birth. Any child I touch becomes a part of me, so that I remember him or her," she added with a tone of disbelief and anguish.

In thinking more about it, Laurine has concluded that "there are many opinions about life and its purpose: how to get the most out of life, how to live a long and productive life and be happy, how to begin life and how to end it, or when it begins. As I have gotten older, I have found that for myself, the answers are sometimes too subtle to decipher except to say that we have our own duty to perform in this life, our individual calling that we need to carry out as best we can, with wisdom and skill. That is the important thing. It has been richly rewarding and

profoundly sad to be involved in the full circle of life. I
have come to be protective and respectful of whatever
way an individual or family decides to make sense of life's
mysteries and to find whatever meaning and happiness
they can."

The ring of fire

During birth, the head pushes on the perineum and
causes a burning sensation referred to by medical people as the ring of fire. In the hospital the vaginal area is
injected with a solution that stops the pain but makes it
smaller and more inclined to tear. As Debora was giving
birth, Laurine sprayed lidocaine onto her gloved finger and
then gently smeared it over the outside of the perineum,
following up with a warm pack. Debora was sitting on the
toilet with the lid down, her feet on Laurine's knees. Laurine carefully eased the head out, then the shoulder, then
the rest of the baby. Her assistant retrieved warm blankets
from the dryer for the mother and baby. The baby's nose
and head were slightly misshapen. The baby was big and
had trouble emerging but was okay. The mother did not
experience tearing and there was little blood.

During the pushing, both in the bathtub and on the
toilet, Debra was helped by her husband, Jeff, who was
a house husband. Laurine thought they had an interesting modern relationship. Jeff liked to build fine furniture and did it at home, so it made sense that he would
raise the children. Laurine appreciated Jeff's commitment

to working with wood because of her own father's quest to construct quality furniture. The young couple's home reminded Laurine of her own childhood upbringing. It was an older home in an established neighborhood with a garage, yard, garden, and lots of birds. The fact that Jeff was to be the house husband did not mean that he was a home body. He and Debora liked to hike and travel. Like Stuart Breisch, Debora was an ER physician. Jeff and Debora both paid attention to their diets. On the day of the birth, the expectant mother and father kicked a soccer ball around the yard for two hours.

When Debora went into labor, so did Jeff, through a phenomenon known as Couvade Syndrome. In ancient Asia, fathers were known to experience several symptoms of pregnancy such as weight gain. It would take the father as much time to shed the extra pounds after delivery as it did his wife. In this case, Jeff was as exhausted after the birth as Debora was. It meant that Jeff needed sleep and was unable to help the baby at this critical time. This did not matter to Laurine, who had learned over the years that the father is usually not much help in the first twenty-four hours anyway. He usually feels a lot of his wife's exhaustion, maybe just for the reason that he has often been up watching over her. This is why Laurine recommends that the pregnant woman arrange to have another woman on hand for the first day or two after birth.

Debora and Jeff would have another baby three years later. This time, as the day of birth approached, Debora had a bout of diarrhea and needed to be given an IV drip. Her friends in the ER had been waiting for a possible call and dashed over in a car to set up the IV tube. For the sake of their three-year-old, Jeff had sprinkled Fairy Dust glitter on his wife's face, which made everyone from the hospital smile. In Africa and Southeast Asia there is an impulse to paint the expectant mother's belly with henna and sprinkle it with herbs. Maybe the impulse to be playful when a baby is born is universal but most often suppressed among strangers at a hospital.

Home is where the heart is

Some families Laurine has visited are of such modest means that she wonders how they can afford a child. One rural couple, ironically Joseph and Mary, had moved in with relatives to be near a midwife through the birth. They had three girls and a fourth girl on the way. She did not ask whether they would have called a little boy Jesus. The family was conservative and frugal, the children home-schooled in such topics as knitting, embroidery, and bottling fruit rather than in science and math. Most of their food came from their garden and barns. They were all slender and shy and seemed ill prepared for the modern world.

When Mary was having her baby, her daughters sat close by in the next room working on hand-crafted toys for the baby. Laurine had given Mary a robe because she did not own one. Mary asked if she could sit in the bathtub, which she thought would be easier to clean up afterward and less of a burden on her hosts than if she gave birth in bed. The bathroom was so small, Laurine could hardly maneuver. The light was dim, so Laurine's assistant lit a candle for illumination. When the child came, that was that. Laurine had another appointment to attend to. The family packed up and traveled back to their rural home and never saw Laurine again.

On the other end of the political spectrum were Tiffany and Mike, who lived in a summer cottage in Big Cottonwood Canyon. They liked living off the grid and were surviving on berries, canned milk, and granola bars. Laurine did not mind helping them but found that her cell phone and pager did not work in the canyon and that she, suddenly the modern woman among them, could not be away from her telephone for long. It would be Tiffany's first baby. Laurine worried that they were so far away from medical help, they would not be able to reach professional assistance if something went wrong. Still, she agreed to help and hoped for the best.

She received a call when Tiffany was in the early stages of labor. After driving up the canyon and finding everything in order, Laurine had to leave to see a woman in West Valley City who was approaching the time of birth. The two couples knew about each other and had empathy for each other's situation. Both had family coming to the rescue. As Laurine drove down the canyon at 11:00 p.m., the moon shining brightly and the weather perfect, she said a prayer of thanks. So far, everything was going alright. When she arrived in West Valley City, everyone was relieved. Curious about how Tiffany was doing, they nevertheless soon turned their attention to the situation at hand because the woman's contractions were not far apart. The baby was born without complications. Soon Laurine was on her way back to see Tiffany and Mike. She arrived at the cabin at four o'clock in the morning. Tiffany's mother was still on her way from Idaho to see her first grandchild born.

Tiffany was dilated to five centimeters, her cervix 90 percent effaced, and the baby was settled at the pelvis (zero station), ready for descent. As it began its birth, Tiffany and her husband calmly sipped herbed tea and talked. With Mike's help, Tiffany assumed various positions as needed, in perfect harmony with the feelings she was having, Laurine noticed. When the sun rose, the canyon was alive with nature. The bed was in an upstairs loft, at the top of a steep flight of stairs. There was no indoor bathroom. At 9:20 a.m. there were smiles all around as a skinny but strong baby arrived into the world. Tiffany felt the rush of adrenaline that mothers experience when the baby makes it first sound—a cry of triumph. Tiffany was not tired at all. Everyone was crying tears of joy.

The baby was six-and-a-half pounds and twenty-one inches long, with black hair that made him look like his father. Tiffany did not need any repair work to her birth canal and there was minimal blood loss. Laurine stayed with her for two hours until her mother came. In fact, Laurine still has the picture in mind of the anxious grandmother being introduced to her shiny new grandson. In the next few years, there would be three more babies born into the family. No longer living in a cabin, they nevertheless moved from the city to a remote area of California where Mike worked in forestry. Laurine gave Tiffany advice on her last pregnancy by telephone. Laurine could not believe her ears when she later heard that Mike and Tiffany had decided to divorce. They had seemed like such a perfect couple. Sometimes these things are for the best, but Laurine had believed in their bucolic fantasy even though she had seen their hardships up close and understood why Mike might want to continue to live in a forest and Tiffany might not. They remain in Laurine's memories as two amazing individuals, for whom the reality of their separation was hard to reconcile with the picture she retains of them in her mind.

Twins and triplets

"Thank goodness for ultrasounds," says Laurine, who has done pre-natal counseling for women carrying twins (five sets) and triplets (two sets). The triplets were brought into the world through C-section surgery because Laurine insisted that Nancy and Arica both visit an obstetrician, where in each case, through ultrasonography (pictures of the inside of the womb), the doctor confirmed that the mother was carrying three individuals at once.

Laurine let them know that carrying and delivering triplets is complicated and risky, as they would learn for
themselves soon enough.

One of the two women, Arica, got married at seventeen years of age to Don, a twenty-one-year-old, and
within two years they had two children, born a year apart.
Laurine liked being around the couple because they were
so loving and respectful of each other and it was convenient to drop in on them since they lived only a mile
away. Arica had tried to breast-feed her first two babies
but gave up because her work schedule was too demanding. When she became pregnant again, she called Laurine
and broke down in tears about this unexpected inconvenience. When Laurine saw her, she knew Arica was too
big too soon and told her to see an obstetrician. The doctor confirmed that she was going to have triplets. "Oh my,
how she grew," Laurine remembers.

They decided that Laurine would do prenatal care
and that Arica would deliver the babies at the University Hospital. Before that, she was to make weekly visits to a nearby clinic. The problem was, she became so
fragile, she could not leave the house without going into
labor. Laurine called in a weekly report on Arica's condition. What she reported, besides vital signs, was that Arica
was huge and had to use a walker to get to the bathroom.
The mother-to-be spent most of her time in a recliner. In
addition to that, the developing babies were active and
gave their mother no rest, leading to the joke that they

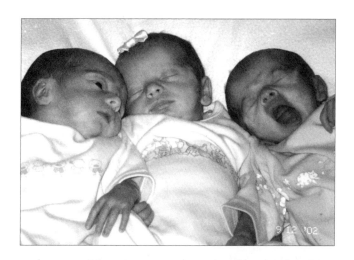

The "triple joys" of Richard and Nancy Nielsen at ten days old in September 2002 and nine years old in 2011. Laurine accompanied Nancy to the hospital and assisted Richard as a birthing coach.

must be boys, which actually turned out to be true. In any case, Arica was uncomfortable throughout her pregnancy.

Finally one day Laurine received the call she had been anticipating when Arica's water broke. Laurine rushed over to find a little leg protruding into the birth canal. *Stay calm,* she remembered telling herself. She could not find Don and had to help Arica to the car herself, where Laurine had her sit on a blue pad on the reclined seat. Laurine could not count how many times she had driven to the University Hospital but had never seen so much traffic as now. She talked to Arica about anything she could think of—the weather, the efficacy of prayer, how cute babies are—to keep the mother's mind distracted and nerves calm. Finally the traffic opened up and they arrived. Laurine accompanied Arica into surgery. Don arrived, nervous but happy. There were three medical teams on hand, one for each baby. Everything went well.

From that point on, Arica and Don were so busy with their five pre-schoolers that time seemed to fly by. Laurine visited several times. At first Arica suffered panic attacks, but she eventually acclimated to the situation. One of the last times Laurine visited, the triplets were two-and-a-half years old. Arica had just put them down on their beds for a nap. Laurine helped Arica unscrew the top portion of a dresser to remove the mirror, further child-proofing their home to keep up with the boys' increasingly higher reach.

There are exceptions to every rule. Most mothers

wear down a bit with each child, but a woman named Lisa was forty-four when she gave birth to her twelfth child, and she seemed to Laurine to be more fit than she had ever been. If anyone should know, it would be Laurine, who had assisted at each of the previous eleven births. The children were so familiar with the midwife that they called her Aunt Laurine. As of the time her last baby arrived, Lisa was exercising and eating well and had the support of her sister-wives in the polygamous family she is a part of. With each birth, the whole family bonded as closely to the baby as did the mother herself. There was no despair on Lisa's part about having a baby in midlife.

Some days are better than others

One time, Laurine was called to help a friend whose daughter, Jody, had been raped by some neighbor boys. The parents went to their Mormon leader for advice, and he recommended an abortion. The young men had prominent fathers, so any news of the crime would be a scandal. Another proposed alternative was to send the girl to live with relatives. In either case, the family would keep quiet. But Jody had already dropped out of school, and after the parents prayed about it, they decided that if she stayed out of sight, it would be the same as if she had left town.

Laurine was surprised, when she arrived, at how close to birth the baby was and how little the family had done to prepare for it. The mother was herself a midwife and informed Laurine that the baby was breeched but not to worry because she had received spiritual reassurance that all would be well. Laurine's heart cried for the young woman. She was a worn-out little girl, completely under the control of her parents, and her parents were not in their right minds. The good news was that Jody was healthy and the baby had good heart tones. But when Laurine touched the girl's back, she knew they had to go to the hospital. With reassurance that she would accompany them, Laurine persuaded the parents to let their daughter seek medical attention. At the hospital, Jody delivered a healthy baby boy via Cesarean section. Laurine felt that the events, as they transpired at the hospital, confirmed her own feeling of spiritual guidance to bring them there. The baby was placed with Jody's grandmother. None of the boys claimed responsibility or were held accountable for their actions.

In another home, the atmosphere was magical as the time came for the birth of the woman's fourth child. As Laurine entered, she could smell the aroma of freshly baked bread. There were two grandmothers on hand to help their daughter or daughter-in-law through the ordeal, and the husband was a perfect coach. The mother, Jenny, looked forward to giving birth. She had treated herself to skin lotions and bubble-bath fragrances. The other children ranged in age from four to seven and were involved and looking forward to the new sister who would even the score in the family to two boys and two girls.

The fourth baby usually takes a little longer, so Laurine was not too concerned when Jenny, although in labor, needed to go to the bathroom and asked if she could have some privacy. Before Laurine knew it, there was a tell-tale sound of pushing from the bathroom. Alarmed at the sound, the five-year-old daughter barged her way into the bathroom to see a bloody cone-shaped projectile emerging from her mother. Confused and excited, the little girl screamed, "Mommy's having a bullet!"

What a contrast between that and another house Laurine was called to, where she was met at the door by a man in a hooded brown robe who said his name was Tony. He explained that he was part of a Nevada commune and they were renting the house in an exclusive Cottonwood Heights area so one of their members could give birth there. They had heard that Utah had better midwives than Nevada. The midwife they had hired was attending to another birth that day, so Laurine was asked to fill in for a pre-natal exam. They walked through a room where several people, including women and children, were dressed in different-colored robes. On their way to the second floor, Tony asked Laurine if she was okay with drugs. She said no, that home births were usually drug-free, to which he replied, "No, no, not for the mother. They would be for us."

She said she did not care but could not imagine what need the family would have for drugs during a birth. Soon she was introduced to a beautiful, long-legged, twenty-five-year-old woman who was in excellent physical condition for an expecting mother. When the exam was over, Laurine left with a prayer in her heart that she would not be called back. Later she talked with the other midwife and learned that the people had chanted and prayed through the labor, that they had taken cocaine, and that Tony had talked about the birth in eugenic terms. The baby weighed eight pounds and was twenty-one inches long. Everyone stayed in the mansion another two weeks and then went back to Nevada.

Laurine stumbled into another unusual scenario one morning at two hours after midnight when she received a frantic call in broken English. She was not sure how the woman had gotten her telephone number. It was another group of visitors to Utah, in this case Mexican emigrants. "I am sorry to call you at this hour, but I am pretty sure my baby is coming," the woman said. Laurine could tell by the mother's voice that she was stressed. "I will be there within the hour," she told the woman, her intuition telling her that she had better hurry.

She dressed in layers because it was raining and loaded her car with equipment. At stops along the way, she studied a map of Murray with the help of a flashlight, almost missing the unpaved cross-street that took her down a hill through various-sized puddles, then right, then left into a drab trailer court where the address told her it was the second trailer on the right. She barely had room to park. She felt apprehensive about being in such a place but got out and tapped on a door where there was no porch light.

Lucinda's eight-year-old daughter opened the door. The oldest of four children, she showed Laurine where to step over snoring bodies in sleeping bags, past another body on a couch. There were three adults in the middle of the floor and two children by the kitchen table. They passed a small room with a washer and dryer and makeshift bed before the girl tapped on a door and then went back to her bed in the washroom. The husband opened the bedroom door. There was just enough room to slide sideways on both sides of a bed, past a built-in closet, a small table, and a huge picture of Marilyn Monroe on the wall.

Lucinda was standing, her face flushed. She was pretty in her long dark hair. Her husband apologized for his brothers in the front room. Laurine assured him that it didn't matter. Assessing the situation, she immediately called her assistant while "Omar" helped her unload the car. Laurine had brought a Doppler ultrasound device, a heating pad, a blood-pressure cuff and stethoscope, oxygen, an Ambu-bag resuscitator, a noise machine, bottles of aromas, and other devices, medicines, and props. She plugged the heating pad into an electrical outlet and started working on charting the woman's vital signs and fetal heart tones.

By the time Kathy, Laurine's assistant, arrived, Lucinda was trembling. Kathy filled the bath with warm water, to which she added a lavender scent. The mother was dilated to six centimeters, 75 percent effacement, and zero station but had a water bulge. The fetal heart tones were at fourteen, meaning they were within normal range and even strong. Lucinda went into the bath tub with a towel for modesty. Kathy turned the noise machine to rain for its soothing effect and poured warm water on Lucinda's stomach from a gallon container. Omar sat on the toilet with the lid closed. Lucinda wondered if she had panicked and called too soon, but Laurine told her it was normal to have a pause in the contractions. Kathy gave the mother a lime popsicle and put towels and blankets in the dryer to heat them. She put Laurine's instruments, gloves, and suction bulb on a blue pad to be moved anywhere they were needed.

The little girl came in to watch, hoping for a little sister. Laurine asked if Lucinda wanted to go to bed, but Lucinda said she felt like pushing. She had barely begun the effort when she thought her water broke. On inspection, Laurine could see flecks of vernix, the waxy substance on a fetus's skin, floating in the water. Her gloves went on and she coached the mother to push again. The baby emerged with a cord around its neck, which Laurine untangled. The cord was long enough to lay the baby on her mother's breast.

"Niña! Niña! Look how beautiful," the mother exclaimed. The baby was not crying but was rooting for its mother's breast. Laurine did a quick evaluation of the baby's skin color, muscle tone, respiration, pulse, and re-flexes and gave it an Apgar score of 8 points out of 10. She asked the little girl in the hallway if she wanted to cut the baby's cord. Omar had been offered this honor and passed on it. In the middle of this ritual, the placenta appeared. Omar went to waken his brothers. "We have a girl!" he shouted. It was so easy sometimes to have a baby. With an underwater birth, there was no mess. The new mother put on a pink nightgown. Laurine examined the baby more closely at the foot of the bed, then checked out the mother. Omar thanked and paid her and her assistant and they left. "That was that," she thought. She and Kathy reached their respective homes in time to make breakfast for their waking families.

Occasionally Laurine would visit someone because she had a premonition she should stop by, which occa-sionally elicited a comment, said with a smile, that it was her fault the client had gotten pregnant because Laurine had thought about them. Sometimes, before every house had a telephone, intuition was all Laurine had to go on. If someone needed to contact her, it could take hours, espe-cially if the potential client did not have Laurine's tele-phone number. For instance, a client in Kaysville sent her husband on the road to the nearest neighbor who had a telephone, from whose house the husband called a rela-tive who lived near Laurine. The relative stopped by Lau-rine's house with a message to come quickly. In this case, Laurine drove over the speed limit and arrived to what she thought was the sound of the woman crying Help! Help! but turned out to be peacocks in the yard. She hurried into the farm house to find Melissa in labor.

Melissa had received her own premonition a few days earlier, but instead of calling the midwife she had gone out and had her hair and nails done. Within an hour of Laurine's arrival, the woman gave birth. Her husband, Jim, proved to be as good a cook and maid as most women and was good with the baby, Laurine could tell. Right from the start, he held the baby to his bare chest and cooed and cawed at it and told it about their farm and current events, the way home-birth advocates of the day suggested. Where most families relied on a grandma or an aunt to help while the mother convalesced, this couple was fine on their own and only called the relatives after Melissa had rested a few days.

Another strong memory from Laurine's repertoire of stories about clients concerns Jeanette, who came from a home that had a lot of children. She could not remember a childhood without responsibility or when she had not looked forward to having a family of her own. She married a shy, sensitive young husband, John, who could not do enough to please her. He worked two jobs and even had a third job he did from their home in Tooele. Laurine had been a midwife for Jeanette's mother. Home birth was nothing new to Jeanette.

Even so, Laurine suggested classes for John and Jeanette since they were first timers, and found herself enjoy-

Some women look great after birth. Knowing the
time was near, Marsha Mangum had her hair and nails
done, as apparently so did the midwife (left) and sister Linda Owen (right), judging from the photograph.
Kim Mangum proved to be an indulgent husband and
father.

ing watching the young couple laugh and bond with each other. When John's mother learned about their plan to give birth at home, she volunteered to be their assistant. It was a typical first birth. Everything was new and wonderful for the young people. Laurine was impressed by the degree of loving support they gave each other. Their first child was a boy. Laurine would help deliver four more children for them, the last of which had Down's syndrome. They had a good pediatrician and knew it would be a Down's baby but wanted to have it anyway, and Jeanette wanted to deliver it at home the way she had given birth to her other children. They welcomed the little girl into their lives with love and patience.

A few years later, John's work took him out of town to Wyoming. His family tried to help out as much as they could. Laurine says she was never around anyone who wanted more out of life or sacrificed more for the sake of his family. But when the Down's baby was three years old, Jeanette decided to leave John and the children. She had been depressed for several years and now felt liberated. To this day, John is still raising the children, but Jeanette will have nothing to do with them. John seems to be content with life. Jeanette said she could not handle the stress of raising a family. Each woman reacts to motherhood differently, and each man reacts to fatherhood differently.

Just when everything is going well

One father called Laurine to say how proud he was

that he had helped his wife have her baby without any outside assistance. Laurine could hear the infant in the background and noticed the high-pitched cry of a premature baby. She asked what color the skin was, how much it weighed, and whether it was nursing, then convinced him to take the baby to the hospital. She later called the hospital and learned that the baby had indeed arrived prematurely and had Strep B. It was hospitalized for ten days. Everything worked out well, but had they not acted soon, the baby probably would have developed pneumonia and perhaps died.

To prevent such disasters, Laurine saw as many as nineteen pregnant women a day at her home for prenatal checkups. When this became too much for her, she set aside two days a week to see patients at her home, with appointments from 10:00 a.m. to 3:00 p.m. one day and from 5:00 p.m. to 7:00 p.m. another day. This schedule seemed to be convenient for anyone's weekly itinerary and was a lot more manageable for Laurine. She also noticed that home births usually occurred at night. There seems to be something in the psyche that triggers evening births. If she could have scheduled the births, they would have all been during the day.

Most of the time when things went wrong and she had to transport a mother to the hospital, it was at night. One evening she was called to Draper, at the south end of the Salt Lake Valley, at about 9:00. As she entered the room, something told her to be cautious. She took the mother's and baby's vital signs. Kate, the mother, apologized because now she thought she had called too soon but said she felt better because Laurine was there. Laurine always stayed at least an hour when she was called to a home in case something happened. It did not seem that Kate was going to have contractions, so they all decided to try to get some sleep. Laurine slept on the couch for an hour. She awoke to quiet voices in Kate's bedroom. She was in labor.

This was Kate's third baby. She said she could not remember the contractions being restricted to one side before. Laurine checked her and found that the baby was in the "left occipito anterior" position. When she checked her again, the baby was "transverse," meaning sideways. Suddenly Kate's water broke and there was an arm and little fist protruding from the birth canal. Laurine pulled on a glove and urged the arm back into the womb and called 911. The ambulance arrived and took Kate to the Jordan Valley Hospital. Laurine rode with her in the ambulance, the husband and grandmother following in a car behind them. They arrived at the hospital's women's center at 3:00 a.m. The ambulance crew alerted the OB staff.

The doctor arrived and soon found a prolapsed chord. He ordered a quick C-section. Because he knew Laurine, he allowed her to join the father in the surgical room. When the doctor lifted the baby onto the warmer, it was limp and not breathing. Laurine walked over and put one hand on the baby's back and another on its chest and gave a little push. The baby breathed and cried. No one in the room made any comment. They were all grateful.

As the saying goes, sometimes you get what you wish for. Over time, Laurine was doing so many births that one day she had five, all within twenty hours. She was getting so that she could go for days without food or sleep. "Youth is great," she says. "As we get older, we need to yield the floor to the next generation." She sometimes thought about the poverty of her profession. She drove a Pinto that rode so low, it sometimes dragged bottom in the snow. Once she was returning from a birth in Midvale, traveling on a side road, when her car stopped. It was 3:00 in the morning. She could see the freeway through the snow. She had a warm coat and boots, so she decided to walk toward the lights in the distance. The snow was up to her knees, and the closer she got to the lights, the farther away they seemed. This was when she decided it was time to get a cellphone.

Looking over her records, Laurine notices a fair number of cases of shoulder dystocia. It means that the shoulders are stuck in the birth canal. Thinking about it, she realizes that home birth is the best remedy for this problem because the birthing mother, without anesthesia, can get onto her hands and knees and let gravity help the baby into place. Sometimes clients had their own remedies for problems. One woman had a Chi Machine that shakes the feet, straightens the spine, and eliminates toxins. The woman thought it would help her recover after giving birth. As it turned out, it took her longer than most to heal, so Laurine considered it a lesson for everyone.

Inside the Co-op, Laurine's work was valued by some, while others thought that anyone can catch a baby and that this is what grandmothers are for. Laurine was sometimes given as little as fifty dollars credit for assisting with a birth. Outside the Co-op, she often did trades or barters, especially with other polygamists. She would help deliver a baby and the husband would lay tile at her house or put on a new roof or shampoo the carpet. This was helpful since the Kingstons had such a large family. When Ronna Hand came to Utah in the 1980s, she taught Laurine the business side of midwifery. Even with this change, Laurine never charged a family more than $850 for her services.

Conclusion

Laurine has received countless expressions of thanks, which she keeps in special boxes devoted to such things. We sat down one day and she shared some of them with me. They brought back memories for her. One was from a young woman from Mexico who, Laurine remembered, lived in a crowded basement apartment with her husband's oldest son. She wrote of the "new confidence and faith" Laurine had given her by showing her how to deliver her baby, Noah, without being anesthetized in a hospital: the "beauty of home birth." The woman commented on the "uplifting light of the [Holy] Spirit that attends you in your work."

Another thank you letter was from a grandmother whose grandchildren and great grandchildren were attended by Laurine. The woman commented on the midwife's "fortitude" to carry on the way she did in the face of adversity, furnishing "guidance and guardianship to expectant mothers and the precious souls that come forth at birth." The woman felt a spiritual connection to Laurine's mission, saying that her success was "my prayer and the prayer of many others."

Laurine finds comfort in such expressions because she often heard rumors that she was the midwife who sent people to the hospital. She knew many of the people on the hospital staffs, so she was sometimes allowed to stay with the birth mother. This looked too cozy to people whose interest in natural birth precluded hospital care when the mother was in real need. Just as Laurine appreciated notes of thanks from mothers, she liked to send thank you notes to people at the hospital for responding quickly and professionally in times of crisis when Laurine was in over her head.

Sometimes the transition to the hospital was rocky. The obstetricians were so used to women receiving epidural treatments that when Laurine brought a woman in, they checked for clots in the uterus without giving the mother anything for the pain. That treatment elicited a different kind of card from Laurine, who referred to this as "legalized rape." She hoped the practitioner would remember this rebuke the next time he saw a home-birth patient. Some doctors, Laurine reported, intentionally exacted retribution against a woman for having attempted a home birth, even performing an episiotomy in one instance without giving anything for the pain. One of Laurine's clients was turned down by five different doctors, all of whom seemed coldly indifferent toward the woman's condition. Whether the doctors felt imposed upon to clean up after someone else and assume liability for someone else's mistake or were simply mean-spirited and wanted to see the midwives put out of business once and for all, Laurine did not know.

Many of the doctors, for instance Stephen D. Ratcliffe, a professor in the Department of Family and Preventive Medicine at the University of Utah School of Medicine, spoke favorably of the "little red-headed polygamist midwife who lives on Redwood Road." One time Laurine was at the University Hospital with a client who wanted a natural birth without drugs and Dr. Ratcliffe asked if he could watch and learn some of Laurine's techniques. He said he was fascinated by the touch and rhythm of the birth.

He was surprised that Laurine was equally interested in what he could teach her. He said he had learned to rely on the knees as one of the most reliable pressure points. He gave her a copy of his book, *Family Practice Obstetrics,* with a personalized inscription on the title page, "as a small token of my respect and affection for all that you do to help people." She treasures this gift from her friend,

Steve, and has found no reason to discount what such people have done to save the lives of mothers while bringing babies into the world under difficult circumstances.

6.

TODAY

✿

What of Laurine in retirement? I spent an afternoon with her on St. Patrick's Day 2011 and noticed that she had on a green blouse. Out the window, the sun was shining. We could see the neighbor's chickens busily scratching in her flower garden. She commented on how much slower she moves at nearly eighty years old than when she was a young woman of only sixty. She attended her last birth as a midwife a little over three years ago. How would she have done things differently, I ask, if she had them to do over again? She would have been more assertive, she says without hesitation, but says it in the sweetest grandmotherly voice. When she was young, it was easy to confuse assertiveness with aggression, she says.

Bonds of love

She remembers hearing once that a mother's relationship with her first son is a reflection of her relationship with her husband. It is true, she says, that her "poor first-born son" was not blessed with a life of ease and comfort, nor were she and Leon in the lap of luxury at the time. They struggled to make ends meet and to have enough energy at the end of the day to spend time with each other. She nursed her son for three weeks and then felt so stressed about returning to work that she stopped breast feeding and returned to her duties at the hospital. During the time she was nursing, she felt like she was wasting time unless she could read a book. Her baby resented this lack of attentiveness and liked to hit the book or newspaper to try to force Laurine to put it down. Laurine tried to hold the reading material out so he could not reach it; then it occurred to her that this behavior showed intelligence on her baby's part and that as the mother, she was missing an opportunity to communicate with him. The importance of nursing went beyond nutrition, she came to understand.

Her husband was fascinated by how the baby's little tongue worked as he swallowed. There were many ways in which Leon was a perfect, doting father. On the other hand, before long he was implementing the same kind of strict oversight he had experienced in his own upbringing, which was the cause of some tension between him and Laurine, whose own father was more indulgent. Laurine thinks she had to learn to love her children unconditionally. It did not come naturally at first. In fact, it took three children before she could fully appreciate the warm, squiggly bundle she held in her arms and not think about what she would otherwise be doing at work.

Her mother often reminded her that each child was born with a different personality. Blenda believed that people were influenced by their pre-existent spirit and that each child should be appreciated for its unique gifts and not seen as a variation on a similar theme. At first, all the future midwife saw in babies was the mess and inconvenience. Only slowly did she begin to apprehend artistic expressions in messiness. It is easier, she says, to see a mess as an impulse toward individuation "in other people's children and in our grandchildren than in our own immediate offspring, for whom we bear the responsibility when they break the living-room vases and spill the kitchen milk."

"I think a life without children would be unimaginable," Laurine comments. Her heart goes out to those who want to have children and cannot have them, even though she knows women who have given birth and never fully recovered, mentally or physically. She says it is not possible to have seven or more children and retain your sanity! Moderation is best. She never liked the complexities of parenthood, although the more she did the tasks associated with parenting, the easier they became. The same applied to midwifery. However, what surprises were in store for her! For instance, she thinks of the time God threw thunderbolts at her family while they were picnicking in the mountains near Huntington in Emery County.

When lightning strikes

It was a beautiful summer day in 1988, and Laurine and Leon were enjoying their extended family, about forty in all, at the Old Folks Flat Campground in Huntington Canyon when a storm moved in, sending the family for cover under some pine trees. The lightning soon followed them, traveling down a tree where two of the Kingstons' five-year-old grandsons, Blake and Zachary, were hit by a "fireball" that threw them about two feet into the air and then dissipated in a puff of smoke. Both boys stopped breathing. Laurine resuscitated Blake and Zachary's mother performed CPR on him. Other family members were hit by lightning and staggered under the power of it. Zachary's Cocker Spaniel, Abbey, was hurt. There was a smell of burned flesh and electricity in the air. One of Laurine's sons drove to the nearest telephone to call for an ambulance. Blake's heart stopped five times during CPR. Eventually, he was helicoptered to Primary Children's Hospital in Salt Lake City, where he received neurosurgery, eye surgery, and physical therapy but recovered.

It was an experience that reminded Laurine of the provisional nature of life. Her daughter said the lightning was "the loudest boom I've ever heard. It stunned everyone. Pine cones and needles came out of the tree like it was raining." It was as if the lightning had tracked them down, Laurine said to herself, although she knew it was crazy to think so. She saw it as a reminder of the impersonal power of nature, over which her training as nurse and midwife had been intended to gain some control but was largely unhelpful at such times. In the moment of crisis, she appreciated the years of study and training that made it possible for her to render aid to a family member in need. But in contests between human beings and Mother Earth, humans are puny and impotent, she realized, and that is why God is needed in the delivery room and elsewhere in medicine.

At the same time, Laurine thought about the hard-earned lessons she had brought to midwifery from her fundamentalist background, where she had seen Co-op and Church leaders too often engage in wishful thinking when colleagues were in need, guaranteeing someone's future health, for instance, and saying it was "God's will" that the individual recover, only to be soon disappointed. She became cautious about stating whether or not someone would recover or even could be cured. She believes that every individual reacts differently to treatment, based on their body chemistry and personality, with so many variables that one can never know what will happen. We are the ones who live in our own bodies, and sometimes we know better than our doctor or priest how things will turn out. She includes herself in that category, as a health professional who can sometimes predict fairly well what will happen but in the end is really playing a game of guesswork.

A hard-earned philosophy

Laurine's upbringing taught her to be frugal, which made her able to empathize with people who have trouble making ends meet. Too many medical people forget that patients have to produce the money to pay for the treatments that are prescribed. In some areas of the world—in Cuba, for instance—there are effective general practitioners who get by with what they have. There are Mennonite doctors and others in this country, too, who do not allow people's reliance on insurance companies and credit cards to dictate the range of treatments they should receive, trying instead to keep medical intervention appropriate to a person's ability to pay.

The most important aspect of anyone's health is what they put in their mouths, Laurine says. She quickly acknowledges the contradiction to what Jesus said about unclean speech, that it is "not that which goeth into the mouth [that] defileth a man; but that which cometh out of the mouth" (Matt. 15:11). She adds her full agreement with Jesus on that point. Where she draws the line, she says, is at Jesus's reluctance to wash his hands before dinner (Luke 11:37-38), the nurse in her dissenting against this lack of hygiene. She chuckles, then turns more serious as she muses over the fact that Jesus ate fish and honeycomb and washed it down with water and wine, from which we might derive a moral about balance and prudence. The point is that, ultimately, if people were smarter about what they ate, we would all have better health.

She tells her grandchildren to begin thinking about how to take care of their health by washing their hands and eating nutritious foods, then asks, "Who is the most important person in the world?" They cheerfully answer, "You are," having been coached to know that the right answer is that "you are the most important." When she tries to correct them, saying "No, you are," they protest that this is what they said, some of them giggling about it. In earnestness, she tells them that when they feel sad, they should find a way to help someone else who is feeling sad as the key to feeling better. It is like taking aspirin.

The other end of life

Laurine volunteered for Hospice Care for two years and heard a cancer patient who had thirteen children tell about baking cookies when she felt depressed. The cookies were not for her but made her feel better. This took Laurine back to her youth in the 900 East neighborhood of Salt Lake City and the Dunford Bakery and Garden Gate Shop, with their mood-altering aromas of cookies and candy. She was not a munch-mouth herself, but it made her happy to bring something home for her brothers and sisters. Later she would treat her own children to root beer and even let the younger ones drink it out of a bottle with a nipple if they wanted to.

It made sense for Laurine to become involved in Hospice Care. Midwives in various times and places have helped prepare bodies for burial. The colonial American midwife, Martha Moore Ballard, wrote of counseling people through old age, disease, and death as well as helping women with birth. A new lay profession in the United States is called a "death midwife," the equivalent of a medical social worker in a hospital. Much of the assistance rendered by Hospice Care people comes from volunteers and others who know how to sit with patients and what to do in an emergency until a registered nurse can be summoned.

In Laurine's case, she took classes about death and dying. It pleased her, after having seen the beginning of life and having spent time with largely non-communicative babies, to be able to carry on conversations at the end of someone's life, as she had done at St. Mark's Hospital at the beginning of her career. "If they needed a good listener, I was the right person," Laurine explained. "Often they need someone to hold their hand and tell them it was alright to die and to present possibilities for the next phase of their existence."

Synesthesia

Laurine could tell what kind of environment she was walking into when she entered a home where someone was dying. She noticed other people's body language. Her mind interpreted the surroundings as a color and texture.

For instance, if a home had recently had a birth in it, it seemed to Laurine to be coated in yellow down. If death was imminent, it might be blue and have a smooth texture. This is a form of synesthesia, which is a psychological condition whereby people associate ideas, words, and numbers with shapes, sounds, colors, smells, and tactile properties. It is considered a gift for some artists, musicians, and poets but considered a disability to people for whom colors, tastes, smells, and shapes are important in their literal form. Think of chefs, perfumers, and engineers, for instance.

Laurine likes the book, *When I Am an Old Woman I Will Wear Purple.* The title makes sense to her synesthetic mind. An anthology of essays on women and aging, its inspiration comes from the poem, "Warning," by Jenny Joseph, in which the speaker imagines she will deal with growing old by learning how to spit, to eat bread and pickles, and to hoard things in boxes. To Laurine, purple brings to mind royalty, especially sovereigns in long satin robes. Older people often seem stately to her, even when they act child-like, and in those moments, she sees them as the nineteen-year-old Charles II of England in camouflage, hiding, or as a *dauphin* in waiting. No matter, just look closely enough and, if you try, you can see a Scarlet Pimpernel winking at you, at least in your imagination.

Tolerance

Laurine has lived long enough and is comfortable

enough with herself that she does not feel the need to sit in judgment of other people. Whatever condescension she may have felt as a child, when she gazed on people outside of the chosen Kingston family, was long ago replaced with an abiding curiosity about other people. She is not homophobic, for instance. She does not pretend to understand the physiology of being gay but thinks people should live the way they feel most comfortable. Hate is a waste of time, and anger takes too much energy, she says. Hate and anger need to be expiated—exorcized and vanquished. The way to heal someone, she says, is to open their eyes and ears to the variety and beauty of nature. "Glory be to God for dappled things," wrote Gerard Manley Hopkins in "Pied Beauty":

> All things counter, original, spare, strange;
>> Whatever is fickle, freckled (who knows how?)
>> With swift, slow; sweet, sour; adazzle, dim;
> He fathers forth whose beauty is past change:
>> Praise him.

"No one is a robot," Laurine likes to repeat when asked about human nature. "We are all different and in need of enlightenment in trying to understand each other." That is not to say that people are justified in whatever they want to think or do, she says, but she finds more guidance for her own life in examples of other people than she sees reason to censor those who are different from her. It may come from having been raised fundamentalist. She still cherishes much of the theology and many of her old acquaintances among the Kingston clan, but she is equally happy that her outlook began to broaden when she decided to become a nurse. She has learned so much from other people, she says. She has felt their love and tenderness, even as she, in return, has experienced the stirrings of emotional connections to them. She is convinced it is not possible to give away love; it always comes back to you. One of the most important aspects of healing is getting rid of the emotional blockage that comes from jealousy and revenge, which are addictive toxins to our psychological health. When we are free of pettiness, we can open our minds to the universe; this is when we begin to solve problems and walk more confidently on the earth. This is especially important for those of us who would like to pass on some wisdom to the upcoming generation, knowing that the world is changing so quickly, we could not possibly have all the answers for our children and grandchildren.

It has not been easy for Laurine to step beyond her upbringing and take public positions on health policies. She joined Toastmasters International to learn how to do what she most dreaded: stand up in public and give a speech without passing out. Women do not speak in public in the Kingston Church, and it would have been heretical to do so. It was terrifying to address an audience of mostly male members of the local Toastmasters affiliate and not assume they resented her. She learned an apho-

Theater professors Michael and Nina Vought of West-minster College were far removed from Laurine in ideology and lifestyle, but they shared her emphasis on family cohesion, eating healthy foods, and natural birth. Laurine says she learned as much from them as they did from her during their brief acquaintance.

rism from television's Dr. Phil that "if you think you know what anyone is thinking, you are wrong." To her surprise, the audience was usually more sympathetic than critical. By taking baby steps, opening her mouth and speaking her prepared lines for starters, she could move an audience to empathy with her life experiences.

The Co-op

The leader of the Davis County Cooperative Society today is Leon's nephew, Paul Kingston, and is the best leader so far, in Laurine's opinion, despite some obvious excesses and flaws. He is intelligent and charismatic. He has some forty wives, according to the *Salt Lake Tribune,* including two half-sisters. "You might call this marriage obsession an addiction," Laurine says. On a recent Fourth of July, Brother Paul's wives gathered in a deserted area near Granite High School and formed a line, their children, about ten each, lined up next to them. Brother Paul arrived, emerged from a car, kissed each wife, and disappeared. An onlooker said the women looked similar, as if sisters. The oldest was about thirty and the youngest was a teenager. The women had on mildly risqué blouses that were tight, with plummeting necklines, apparently reflecting some subtle competition for their husband's attention, which he apparently responds to with appreciation.

The almost military precision accompanying Brother Paul's review of his wives reflects his love of orderliness.

Even though he is rigid in schedules and business fore-casts, Laurine says he is more willing than his predecessors to listen and learn from other people and explore new ways of doing things. The Co-op is doing well. The blood, sweat, and tears of the past have paid off, at least in terms of financial security. On the other hand, the members are all from the same die and are uniformly quiet, obedient, and giving. "They give and give and ask nothing in return," Laurine comments. "They eat healthy foods and avoid what they consider to be poisons," in keeping with their Mormon cousins. They have come to respect education and now encourage it. The Co-op markets products in such far-flung destinations as China. They are able to point out that they are communists with a small "c." They are also, according to their comments about themselves, "true Christians" and "a pure strain of Mormonism."

Laurine confronted Brother Ortell one time about intermarriage, explaining that she had medical concerns about it. He compared marriage to climbing a mountain and said it was easy to keep your footing at the base, but the higher you climbed, the narrower the mountain became and the harder to keep from falling off the top. For the general population, it is fine to look far and wide for marriage partners, but this will not do for the Kingston family, according to Brother Ortell's response. This satisfied Laurine for a while. She felt fine about it, thinking that in the field of animal husbandry, sometimes you want hybrid vigor and sometimes you want purebred stock. But over time, the rationale came to make less sense to her. She has not encouraged her own children to marry within the family, for instance.

When Laurine had this conversation with Brother Ortell, she was still naive in wanting to be a good Co-op member and to please her leader even though Ortell was an old childhood friend. She reacted to the outside world by compartmentalizing what she was learning and what she had been previously taught, each system seeming logically consistent within itself. Only when the assumptions of one worldview spilled over into the unquestioned habits of the other way of approaching life did she experience cognitive dissonance, and in that sense, it was like walking through the looking glass every morning. It may have been fortuitous that nursing was less philosophically oriented than some other fields of medicine; in some aspects it was a skilled trade she could perform and let others make decisions about epistemology and ethics. But ultimately, medicine was the catalyst for Laurine's entry into the larger world, which she nevertheless entered on her own terms through the synthesis of two worlds rather than by completely repudiating either one of them. For a long time, she was in a kind of cocoon, acclimating to the outside world before entering it completely.

Family ties

At least twice a month, Leon, Laurine, Rowenna, and

all their children get together. They have a lot to talk about. To someone unaccustomed to large families, their catch-up time would seem like chaos. It includes the exchange of youngsters' clothes that have become too small for them and toys that have become uninteresting. This goes on for hours. Those who live in Salt Lake City drop in more often, but the semi-monthly "party day" is something the children and grandchildren hate to miss. During the day, they migrate from one house to the other. Laurine's home is usually quieter. Rowenna's son-in-law owns a reception center close by, which the family sometimes makes use of. It is easy for the children to get along, with memories of the time they all lived together in the same house.

They laugh about such incidents as the time Laurine promised two girls jelly beans if they would help with some chores. When they were done and Laurine found there was only one jelly bean left in the bowl, she cut it in half and gave each daughter a piece. They looked at each other as if to say, "you've got to be kidding me," although they did not say it. How true, the line from Shakespeare, that "all these woes shall serve for sweet discourses in our time to come," is the sentiment that comes to mind when Laurine thinks of their once Spartan ways.

The children turn to Laurine for advice because she has a good track record in that area. She has a secret. She says a quick prayer, then projects her mind twenty years from the present and asks if the decision will matter in twenty years. If not, she says, "Go ask your father." He

The distinguished-looking Ekstrom siblings posing in 2001 at the Kingston house on Redwood Road. Standing are brothers Vernal, Alton, and Virgil; sitting are sisters Rowenna, Laurine, and Sheila. Laurine, who was seventy years old at the time, is the oldest, seventeen years older than Sheila.

actually has an acute sense for what is needed in the here and now. Back when she had the life of a mother or baby in her hands and had to make split-second decisions, she was always able to think clearly and rationally despite the adrenaline rush. Rather than make her faint the way danger affects some people, the adrenaline had a way of sharpening her mind and focusing her attention on the mother's health risks, the father's emotional stability, and the couple's financial future. In that context, the decision was usually obvious.

Fasting and prayer

These days, if a decision requires long-term thought, Laurine turns to what she learned from her husband's family and goes on a fast. This is how she made the decision to marry Leon, going a full eight days without nourishment. How is this possible? people want to know when they hear about it. She acknowledges that it is a mysterious practice and knows it makes some people feel exhausted, their minds muddled, but says it has the opposite effect on her. She knows that fasting is not explicitly recommended by the Bible and that not all Christians engage in it. The Puritan founders of America held fast days, among which Thanksgiving was their favorite, indicating that abstinence from food and water was only one aspect of the practice. It may be worth mentioning that early Mormon pronouncements on the topic came from the same contradictory wellspring, the Doctrine and Covenants commanding adherents to "let thy food be prepared with singleness of heart that thy fasting may be perfect" (59:13).

Laurine does not feel that fasting is required of her, but truth be told, she is ascetic in her religious practices. She is careful to not overeat, feeling that what her body does not need may be needed by others. She abstains from wine and sweets. She prefers a salad over meat dishes. Her view of life leans in the direction of duty, frugality, and orderliness more than pleasure or aesthetic pursuits. That she can go eight days without food is a testament to her chosen lifestyle, but there are other hints of it. For instance, when she was practicing midwifery, she would sometimes go several days without sleep, accepting this regimen as part of her calling. She would go hours without visiting the toilet because she did not want to interrupt the expectant mother's labor. When a woman had delivered her baby and Laurine was free to go, she would breathe the outside air, look up in the sky, and say, "I am doing what you told me. I am following the path." Despite this confidence in her calling, she has always shunned attention and avoided the public square except when her intensity of feelings about midwifery, the direction of the Kingston group, and the future of her posterity have compelled her to.

Laurine believes that we are so complex, we cannot even comprehend the interaction of mind, body, and soul that contributes to our overall health—the basis of the holistic approach to medicine she learned from Dr. Rulon Allred. Sometimes people need counseling, other times they need medicine, and sometimes they need prayer. Sometimes the physician should humble himself through fasting. When Laurine does so, she listens for quiet promptings. Once when she was fasting, she felt she was being told to drink a glass of lemon water. It was two o'clock in the afternoon and she thought she was being tempted. When the prompt came again, she submitted to it. She then felt the lemon water move through her body to enliven every cell, and this convinced her it was something she had needed.

In the context of our country's Puritan heritage, Laurine's reliance on inspiration brings to mind Anne Hutchinson, who is a hero in the telling of our national story but was, at the time, someone who was thrown out in the snow for relying on inspiration. Mormonism inherited her view of personal revelation trumping scripture, while mainline Protestant churches rejected the notion and found reliance on personal feelings to be dangerous. What does Laurine think of the controversy? She says she does not act hastily if her sources contradict each other, among which she counts official statements on scripture, sermons that have been delivered by the numbered brothers in her tradition, her own rationalistic deductions, and the views of her family and clients. If she is in tune with what she feels are the promptings of the Holy Spirit, she is usually in harmony with all of the above. When not, she proceeds carefully and may keep her head down, vouchsafing her opinion to no one at the time.

She says she overdid the fasting when she was young, going without food when she was pregnant or nursing. This was the result of a misguided ego, she has concluded. When asked, she admits she has never seen a healing come about as the result of fasting. She knows of cases of people who have thought they were cured by fasting and then died. Her mother was a victim of a fanatic attachment to the practice. Still, Laurine feels compelled to fast. Nothing can be so bad, she says, as something applied in the wrong way. She has mixed feelings about the co-op's teaching that one should go three days without food or water, followed by three days with only water and no food. This is right for an advanced practitioner but not for children or neophytes. Everyone should choose for herself, Laurine believes, even though she feels the teaching is basically a good one.

There is something more fundamental than whether or not to fast. It is—and in this she says she is part of a growing trend in the world—in keeping with a quest for authenticity. It is a good thing that people stand back and ask themselves whether the path they are on is a good one. How long should someone submit to a regimen for the sake of self-discipline, and at what point should someone admit it is not working and not to their liking and they should turn to something else? Laurine has some

regrets, as anyone does, at having let opportunities to disagree with authority figures pass in order not to be impo-
lite. In this, she learned from her sister-wife, Rowenna,
how to politely disagree or, if the officious individual per-
sists, let him know he is out of line.

Aging

As Laurine gets older, she is more grateful than ever
before to have her family around her. She and Leon and
one of their sons eat at the same table every day and enjoy
each other's company. Their home is open to almost anyone, although Laurine has learned to say no to people
who come asking for favors. It took her a long time to
realize she had the right to make time for herself or to
turn down requests for help with good causes. Her son
needs attention. In his thirties he was diagnosed with
astrocytoma—subependymal giant cell astrocytoma, to
be exact—a form of brain tumor that, although it proved
to be benign, damaged his short-term memory. He works
at a business that understands his condition, where he is
appreciated for his hard work, in keeping with what he
has learned at the Co-op. He likes giving his money to
the Co-op.

Laurine's hope is that she can age gracefully as she
is dragged kicking and screaming into old age. Sometimes she fantasizes about what it will be like beyond the
veil, where she assumes she will be busy even though
the demand for midwives will be presumably less than

on earth. It depends on one's eschatological view. For instance, if heaven is like an Elysian Field, as the Greeks imagined it would be, there might still be midwives! Or maybe in heaven, people like Laurine will prepare spirits for their entry into mortality. Her secret wish is to learn how to fly and leave the harp playing to others.

Recently she had her hip replaced. She is not a good hospital patient. She pled for privacy and told her friends to stay away. She did not want flowers, would not answer the phone, and would not engage in small talk. Nor did she ask the Co-op leader's permission this time or inform him of her surgery. She thinks he may as well consult her as for her to consult him, although she would not let their differences interfere with serious consideration of his advice, just as she would hope he would not dismiss her views because she is a woman.

Trending toward the feminine

Laurine believes the world is becoming more spiritual. This is optimistic, she knows, and one has to put the world's ideological conflicts aside to see people interacting with each other across vast distances, discussing ways to bring mutual understanding, to help the environment, to be fair and just. There is a lot to be pleased with. She looks forward to the day when fundamentalists will be granted the same rights in the United States as everyone else. She imagines a future when natural birth and midwifery will thrive. She watches her own children go about their lives without fear of persecution and is pleased. She marvels at the dissemination of intelligence over the Internet. Everything is moving too quickly for older people, she concludes. She feels like collapsing under the weight of it except that it is so exciting, she is not yet content to let the world pass her by.

She is glad she is a woman. She enjoys giving comfort to other people, which may be driven in part by hormones and instincts. She chose a particularly female profession in which the vaunted strengths of men, including those of the prophet himself, often succumb to wobbly knees in comparison to the stamina of the women. It takes a strong constitution to assist in a birth. It takes patience, which doctors often lack, as well as empathy, trust, and a willingness to get close enough to a woman to learn her particular circumstances. This is why there will always be a need for midwives.

What an interesting combination of fundamentalism and feminism Laurine is! She continues to speak positively about the Co-op's leaders. She follows the Church's basic guidelines and respects the appointed men as long as their advice is sensible. When the men infringe on her right to agree or disagree with them, she objects. She is happy to be led, and thinks of her ancestor Annice McArthur in Mt. Pleasant in the 1870s, holding on to the cow's tail, but she refuses to be driven. It makes her the most improbable liberal, sympathizing with the Mormon candidate, Mitt Romney, for instance, but voting for Barack Obama;

opposing abortion, but favoring a woman's right to choose.

There are other ways in which she is an enigma in that she speaks the language of the medical profession while still viewing herself as an outsider. Even with Certified Midwife credentials, she aligns herself with lay practitioners because she sympathizes with underdogs. She likes to joke about why obstetricians say they practice medicine. It is because they are not yet proficient and are still practicing.

When Ronna Hand came to Utah in the 1970s, she and Laurine became instant friends. Laurine liked her poise around doctors. When Ronna heard that an obstetrician opposed her methods, she would invite him to lunch and proceed to both charm and educate him. It helped that she was attractive and had nursing experience. Her success was a revelation to Laurine, who decided she, too, would venture out into the world when opportunities presented themselves. It pleased her to see the founding in 1980 of the Utah School of Midwifery, now the Midwives College of Utah, by Dianne Bjarnson, a woman who had studied herbology at the School of Natural Healing in Springville, Utah, and had begun her apprenticeship under Ronna. Bjarnson says "the Lord guided me to this profession." The midwives college now has about 150 students.

Laurine is enthusiastic about seeing young midwives receive comprehensive education and apprenticeships, as well as seeing the camaraderie these girls develop as they

Laurine's midwife apprentices celebrating a milestone at a Salt Lake City restaurant. They are, from right, Tami Pugh, Kim Smith, and Kristi Ridd; second from left, Mary Ann Jordan.

progress through a structured curriculum. Laurine has always said that, as proud as she was to be a licensed practical nurse, she always considered it more important "to be a professional human being." Instead of getting a degree in the humanities, by studying what other people have done for the human race, students of midwifery are required to delve deeply into their souls and exercise their own personal humanity, while hopefully not neglecting the study of history and culture either. As Laurine has said, it is the equivalent of being a river flowing to the sea and contributing to farms and trees and everything along the way, while taking back little or nothing.

It is a profession that also entails adventure and courage. As Professor Ulrich wrote in *A Midwife's Tale* about her protagonist:

> Martha Ballard crossed the river in a canoe on December 2, pushing through ice in several places. On December 30 of another year, summoned by a woman in labor, she walked across, almost reaching shore before breaking through to her waist at Sewall's Eddy. She dragged herself out, mounted a neighbor's horse, and rode dripping to the delivery. Necessity and a fickle river cultivated a kind of bravado ... "People Crost the river on a Cake of ice, ..." Martha wrote on December 15 of one year. On April 1 of another she reported walking across on the ice after breakfast, adding drily in the margin of the day's entry, "the river opened at 4 hour pm." (4)

In one instance, the eighteenth-century midwife's

account sounds very much like Kingston's experience where Ballard wrote in her diary that

> a Larg tree blew up by the roots before me which Caused my hors to spring back & my life was spared. Great & marvillous are thy sparing mercies O God. I was assisted over the fallen tree by Mr Hains. Went on. Soon Came to a stream. The Bridg was gone. Mr Hewin took the rains waded thro & led the horse. Assisted by the same allmighty power I got safe thro & arivd unhurt. (5-6)

The same hardship and heroism exist in Laurine's narratives, just that they have a modern setting. Laurine sometimes struggles to articulate the feelings she has experienced over women she has accompanied to death's door and back, for experiences she says she would not have believed unless she had experienced them herself, for God's hand in her life—the gift of being able to live with purpose and for lessons learned and wisdom acquired in small portions. All in all, it has been a good life—an idiosyncratic Utah life that perhaps only those who live here can fully understand. Most people in Utah will feel a kinship with the people she describes and the heritage she comes from, including midwifery as much as any other iconic symbol from religion, pioneering, polygamy, or the strong female role models who were as much a part of the colonization of the West as covered wagons, temples, and irrigation systems bringing water from the mountains to valley floors.

References

Burgess, Victoria D. *Home Birth and Midwifery in Utah.* Salt Lake City: By the author, 2008.

Palmer, Douglas D. "Lightning Struck the Family, Too," *The Deseret News,* July 7, 1988, B-1, 13.

Ulrich, Laurel Thatcher. *A Midwife's Tale: The Life of Martha Ballard, Based on Her Diary, 1785-1812.* New York: Vintage Books, 1991.

Index

abortion, 251

Allred, Rulon, 104, 138, 186-87; holistic approach, 80, 246; murdered, 1; proposes to Laurine, 79; treats Laurine's son for night terrors, 128-29; treats swollen toe, 86-87

American College of Nurse Midwives, 138

Anabaptists, 133

Anderson, L. Roland, Utah District Attorney, 103

antidotes, *see* home remedies

Apache death grip, method of child discipline, 120

Apgar score, 215

Apostolic United Brethren, 1, 80; *see also* Allred, Rulon

Arrington, Leonard, xii

Aschliman, Marie, 98

Atomic Energy Commission, ix

Atwood, Vesta, *see* Kingston, Vesta

automobiles, 1940 Plymouth, 92; Laurine learns to drive, 93;

Model T, 92; Nash Rambler, 92; *see also* Model T Ford

Ballard, Martha Moore, colonial midwife, 234, 253-54

Bannock tribe, 13, 20

Bear Lake, 18

Ben Lomond Hotel, 29

Berlin, Germany, x, xiii

beta-endorphin, 142

Big Cottonwood Canyon, 203

Big Love, 118

bigamy, *see* polygamy

birth, euphoria, xi, 113-14, 137, 180, 142-43, 151-52; family's involvement, xiii, 27, 59, 151, 157, 209, 214; jaundice, x, 194; meconium aspiration, 188, 197; miscarriage, 18, 31; most often in evening hours, 219, 221; pain, 1, 31, 114, 137, 141-42, 159, 173-74, 188, 190-91, 194, 200, 223-24; placenta previa (bleeding), 101, 139, 163, 174, 191, 204; prolapsed um-